New and C

New and Collected Poems

Dannie Abse

HUTCHINSON
LONDON

First published in 2003 by Hutchinson

1 3 5 7 9 10 8 6 4 2

White Coat, Purple Coat: Collected Poems 1948-1988 first published by Hutchinson in 1989
Remembrance of Crimes Past first published by Hutchinson in 1990
On the Evening Road first published by Hutchinson in 1994
Arcadia, One Mile first published by Hutchinson in 1998

Hutchinson
The Random House Group Limited
20 Vauxhall Bridge Road, London SW1V 2SA

Random House Australia (Pty) Limited
20 Alfred Street, Milsons Point, Sydney
New South Wales 2061, Australia

Random House New Zealand Limited
18 Poland Road, Glenfield,
Auckland 10, New Zealand

Random House (Pty) Limited
Endulini, 5a Jubilee Road
Parktown 2193, South Africa

The Random House Group Limited Reg. 954009

www.randomhouse.co.uk

A CIP catalogue record for this book is available
from the British Library

Papers used by Random House are natural, recyclable products made from wood grown in sustainable forests. The manufacturing processes conform to the environmental regulations of the country of origin

Typeset by MATS, Southend, Essex
Printed and bound in Great Britain by
Biddles Ltd, Guildford and King's Lynn

ISBN 0 09 179518 4

Author's note

The majority of poems I have published while and since I was a medical student in the post-war years are collected here, along with new poems written after the publication of *Arcadia, One Mile* (1998). Three of these latter poems first appeared in the pamphlet, *Encounters* (Hearing Eye, 2000): 'A Prayer in the Waiting Room' was commissioned by the Hyphen 21 project, *Poems for Doctors' Waiting Rooms*; the Cini Foundation in Venice commissioned the poem, 'Snapshot of Ruskin in Venice'.

Acknowledgements are also owed for the new poems to the editors of *Ambit*; *Acumen*; *After Pushkin* (The Folio Society); *Jewish Quarterly*; *The Literary Review* (USA); *London Magazine*; *Poetry Ireland*; *PN Review*; *Poetry Review*; *Poetry Wales*; *Rattapolax* (USA); *Sightlines* (Vintage) and *Slope 8*. 'The Yellow Bird', much revised, is based on a poem of that title which I wrote in 1945 and which was published in *After Every Green Thing* (Hutchinson, 1948). Over the last year I have also made minor revisions to 'Tyrant' (1954) and to 'The Abandoned' (1957). 'The Relic' is a variation of Ewald Osers's translation of 'Paradise Lost' by J. Seifert, *The Selected Poetry of Jaroslav Seifert* (Macmillan, 1986). 'The Appointment' is a distorted mirror image of Brecht's 'Changing the Wheel' translated by Michael Hamburger, *Modern European Verse* (Vista Books, 1965) and in 'Domestic' I've stolen a few lines from 'The Claim' by T. Carmi, (Penguin Modern Poets, 1976).

These *New and Collected Poems* are dedicated with gratitude to my most sympathetic reader, Joan Abse.

Now I can do no better than quote Primo Levi: 'The pleasure of seeing your creature grow, beam after beam, bolt after bolt, solid, necessary, suited to its purpose; and when it's finished you look at it and you think that perhaps it will live longer than you, and perhaps it will be of use to someone you don't know, who doesn't know you. Maybe as an old man, you'll be able to come back and look at it, and it will seem beautiful, and it doesn't really matter so much that it will seem beautiful only to you, and you can say to yourself, "Maybe another man wouldn't have brought it off."'

Contents

Part Two: New Poems 1998-2002

Part One

Collected Poems

1948-1998

Toy Soldiers

Toy soldiers are marching, hurrah, hurrah,
over a tablecloth land.
The eyes of the child are crazy, crazy,
as he raises his terrible hand.

Toy soldiers are broken, hurrah, hurrah,
their tin hearts slowly die.
The child's right eye is gleaming, gleaming,
but the left eye starts to cry.

Blow your toy bugle, child, blow,
let imaginary cannons boom.
Use the model truck as a hearse,
the Swan matchbox as a tomb.

Blow your toy bugle, child, blow,
poppy days need not endure,
the factory is making new soldiers
and father will buy you more.

The Uninvited

They came into our lives unasked for.
There was light momentarily, a flicker of wings,
a dance, a voice, and then they went out
again, like a light, leaving us not so much
in darkness, but in a different place
and alone as never before.

So we have been changed
and our vision no longer what it was,
and our hopes no longer what they were;
so a piece of us has gone out with them also,
a cold dream subtracted without malice,

the weight of another world added also,
and we did not ask, we did not ask ever
for those who stood smiling
and with flowers before the open door.

We did not beckon them in, they came in uninvited,
the sunset pouring from their shoulders,
so they walked through us as they would through water,
and we are here, in a different place,
changed and incredibly alone,
and we did not know, we do not know ever.

Epithalamion

Singing, today I married my white girl
beautiful in a barley field.
Green on thy finger a grass blade curled,
so with this ring I thee wed, I thee wed,
and send our love to the loveless world
of all the living and all the dead.

Now, no more than vulnerable human,
we, more than one, less than two,
are nearly ourselves in a barley field –
and only love is the rent that's due
though the bailiffs of time return anew
to all the living but not the dead.

Shipwrecked, the sun sinks down harbours
of a sky, unloads its liquid cargoes
of marigolds, and I and my white girl
lie still in the barley – who else wishes
to speak, what more can be said
by all the living against all the dead?

Come then all you wedding guests:
green ghost of trees, gold of barley,
you blackbird priests in the field,
you wind that shakes the pansy head
fluttering on a stalk like a butterfly;
come the living and come the dead.

Listen flowers, birds, winds, worlds,
tell all today that I married
more than a white girl in the barley –
for today I took to my human bed
flower and bird and wind and world,
and all the living and all the dead.

Song for Dov Shamir

Working is another way of praying.
You plant in Israel the soul of a tree.
You plant in the desert the spirit of gardens.

Praying is another way of singing.
You plant in the tree the soul of lemons.
You plant in the gardens the spirit of roses.

Singing is another way of loving.
You plant in the lemons the spirit of your son.
You plant in the roses the soul of your daughter.

Loving is another way of living.
You plant in your daughter the spirit of Israel.
You plant in your son the soul of the desert.

1948

Letter to Alex Comfort

Alex, perhaps a colour of which neither of us had dreamt
may appear in the test-tube with God knows what
    admonition.
Ehrlich, certainly, was one who broke down the mental
    doors,
yet only after his six hundred and sixth attempt.

Koch also, painfully, and with true German thoroughness,
eliminated the impossible to prove that too many of us
are dying from the same disease. Visible, on the slide
at last – Death – and the thin bacilli of an ancient distress.

Still I, myself, don't like Germans, but prefer the unkempt
voyagers who, like butterflies drunk with suns,
can only totter crookedly in the dazed air
to reach, charmingly, their destination as if by accident.

That Greek one, then, is my hero who watched the bath water
rise above his navel, and rushed out naked, 'I found it,
I found it' into the street in all his shining and forgot
that others would only stare at his genitals.
    What laughter!

Or Newton, leaning in Woolsthorpe against the garden wall,
forgot his indigestion and all such trivialities,
but gaped up at heaven in just surprise, and, with
true gravity, witnessed the vertical apple fall.

O what a marvellous observation! Who would have
    reckoned
that such a pedestrian miracle could alter history,
that, henceforward, everyone must fall, whatever
their rank, at thirty-two feet per second, per second?

You too, I know, have waited for doors to fly open, played
with your cold chemicals, written long letters
to the Press; listened to the truth afraid, and dug deep
into the wriggling earth for a rainbow with an honest spade.

But nothing rises. Neither spectres, nor oil, nor love.
And the old professor must think you mad, Alex, as you rehearse
poems in the laboratory like vows, and curse those clever scientists
who dissect away the wings and haggard heart from the dove.

Portrait of a Marriage

To the suburban house you return again
with a new hat and the stammering discourse
of mild rebellion. You dare not entertain
questions like – Can I start again? Seek divorce?
Because now, middle-aged, you would gain
nothing but insecurity and remorse,
all the might-have-beens crying in the brain.

It was false even before the first caress
but how you strove to make it true,
fouling silence, talking louder to suppress
the lie that somehow grew and grew,
as you hid each new distress
behind the photograph of the smile and you
less than radiant in your wedding dress.

And, in the stabbed evenings, when the sun
died, by appointment, in its Joseph's coat,
you asked help from that anyone
whose million edition pen could write
romantic novels to overcome
the truth of the lonely all about,
the taste of nothing on your tongue.

Now, one year's gone since your clumsy honeymoon
and he talks to you behind an unlocked door;
again your artificial smile alone
floats between the ceiling and the floor,
like some quiet heartbreak, almost to condone
what, after all, others too must slow endure,
the clock, the unhappiness, the civilized bore.

Until those untamed voices in this tidy room
weirdly rise again to show
what is your and your husband's doom,
the dullness you should never know,
the silent piano in the gloom,
the cut-glass vases you endow
with flowers, to disguise this here and now.

Albert

Albert loved dogs mostly, though this was absurd
for they always slouched away when he touched their fur,
but once, perching on his shoulder, alighted a bird;

a bird alive as fire and magical as that day
when clear-eyed Héloïse met Peter Abelard.
Though cats followed him, the bird never flew away.

And dogs pursued the cats which hunted the bird.
Albert loved dogs deeply but was jealously hurt
that they pursued him merely because of the bird;

the bird alive as fire and magical as that day.
So one morning he rose and murdered the bird.
But then the cats vanished and the dogs went away.

Albert hated dogs after, though this was absurd.

Leaving Cardiff

I wait in the evening air.
Sea-birds drop down to the sea.
I prepare to sail from where
the docks' derelictions are.

I stand on the deck and stare,
slack hammocks of waves below,
while black shapes upon the pier
make the furthest star seem near.

Now the funnel's negations blow
and my eyes, like spaces, fill,
and the knots of water flow,
pump to my eyes and spill.

For what *who* would choose to go
when *who* sailing made no choice?
Not for one second, I know,
can I be the same man twice.

The straw-coloured flames flare still,
spokes over the long horizon,
and the boats under the hill
of Penarth unload and move on.

The Mountaineers

Despite the drums we were ready to go.
The natives warned us shaking their spears.
Soon we'd look down on them a mile below
rather as Icarus, so many poets ago,
waved to those shy, forlorn ones, dumb on a thumbnail field.
We started easily but oh the climb was slow.

Above us, the grey perilous rocks like our pride
rose higher and higher – broken teeth of the mountain –
while below the dizzy cliffs, the tipsy angles signified
breathless vertigo and falling possible suicide.
So we climbed on, roped together. At the night camps
our voices babel yet our journey glorified.

The soul too has altitudes and the great birds fly
over. All the summer long we climbed higher,
crag above crag under a copper sulphate sky,
peak above peak singing of the deserted, shy,
inconsolable ones. Still we climb to the chandelier stars
and the more we sing the more we die.

So ascending in that high Sinai of the air,
in space and canyons of the spirit, we lost ourselves
amongst the animals of the mountain – the terrible stare
of self meeting itself – and no one would dare
return, descend to that most flat and average world.
Rather, we made a small faith out of a tall despair.

Shakespeare, Milton, Wordsworth, came this way
near the lonely precipice, their faces gold
in the marigold sunset. But they could never stay
under the hurricane tree so climbed to allay
that voice which cried: 'You may never climb again.'
Our faces too are gold but our feet are clay.

We discovered more than footprints in the snow,
more than mountain ghost, more than desolate glory,
yet now, looking down, we see nothing below
except wind, steaming ice, floating mist – and so
silently, sadly, we follow higher the rare songs of oxygen.
The more we climb the further we have to go.

Letter to *The Times*

Sir, I have various complaints to make.
The roses, first. When they are ripped
from the earth expiring, we sigh for them,
prescribe tap-water, aspirin, and salt.
But when we lie down under the same earth,
in a dry silly box, do they revive us?
Their odour of rose-ghosts does not change
at all, and they continue to call out
in their red and white morse the old, old
messages as if nothing had happened. Again,
consider trees. My God, the impresario
trees. Just try, Sir, just try to cut one down
in Fitzjohn's Avenue at three o'clock
in the ordinary afternoon. You will be
prosecuted. Soon the Householders will arrange
themselves into a deranged *mob*. They'll grow
Hitler moustaches, Mussolini chins. Frightful,
and write oathy letters to the Council,
naming you *tree-criminal*. Yet tell me, when

the bombs met their shadows in London,
amidst the ruins of voices, did one tree, just one
tree write an angry note in its sly green ink?
No, they only dropped faded tears in autumn
selfishly thinking of their own hamadryads . . .
BUSINESS AS USUAL was, and is, their trite
slogan. Away then with trees and roses.
They are inhuman. Away also with rivers:
the disgusting Ganges bleeding from Brahma's
big toe; the Rubicon cause of a Civil War;
the Acheron, River of Sorrows; Tiber that drowned
Horatius the One-Eyed; the sweating Rhône,
Rhine, Don, and the vulgar Volga, not to
mention the garrulous Mississippi with its
blatant river-smell. Even the English
rivers can do no more than reflect inverted
values, turn chaste swans upside down
like so many flies on the roof of the waters.
Swans, however, *cannot* swim upside down.
At least, I have never seen them. Is this distortion
of truth deliberate? Has ever one river,
one river, Sir, written eulogies of waterfalls
to plead for the reprieve of Mankind? And stars,
so indifferent and delinquent, stars which we have
decorated with glittering adjectives more numerous
than those bestowed on Helen's eyes – do they
warn us when they fall? Not a hint.
Not a star-wink. They are even too lazy
to shine when we are most awake. Creatures
of night, they are probably up to immoral
purposes. You can't trust a star, that's sure.

So when the greenfly is in the rose,
and the dragonfly drops its shadow in the river;
when the axe hides in the tree with its listening
shriek, and clouds gag the starlight
with grey handkerchiefs – I contend, Sir,
that we should pity them no more,
but concern ourselves with more natural things.

Duality

Twice upon a time,
there was a man who had two faces,
two faces but one profile:
not Jekyll and Hyde, not good and bad,
and if one were cut, the other would bleed –
two faces different as hot and cold.

At night, hung on the hooks on the wall
above that man's minatory head,
one wants brass where one wants gold,
one sees white and one sees black,
and one mouth eats the other
until the second sweet mouth bites back.

They dream their separate dreams
hanging on the wall above the bed.
The first voice cries: 'He's not what he seems,'
but the second one sighs: 'He is what he is,'
then one shouts 'wine' and the other screams 'bread',
and so they will all his raving days
until they die on his double-crossed head.

At signposts he must wear them both.
Each would go their separate ways
as the East or the West wind blows –
and dark and light they both would praise,
but one would melt, the other one freeze.

I am that man twice upon this time:
my two voices sing to make one rhyme.
Death I love and Death I hate,
(I'll be with you soon and late).
Love I love and Love I loathe
God I mock and God I prove,
yes, myself I kill, myself I save.

Now, now, I hang these masks on the wall.
Oh Time, take one and leave me all
lest four tears from two eyes fall.

The Trial

The heads around the table disagree,
some say hang him from the gallows tree.

Some say high and some say low
to swing, swing, swing, when the free winds blow.

I wanted to be myself, no more,
so I screwed off the face that I always wore,

I pulled out the nails one by one –
I'd have given that face to anyone.

For those vile features were hardly mine;
to wear another's face is a spiritual crime.

Why, imagine the night when I would wed
to kiss with wrong lips in the bridal bed . . .

But now the crowd screams loud in mockery:
Oh string him up from the gallows tree.

Silence! the Judge commands, or I'll clear the court,
to hang a man up is not a sport –

though some say high and some say low
to swing, swing, swing, when the free winds blow.

Prisoner, allow me once more to ask:
what did you do with your own pure mask?

I told you, your honour, I threw it away,
it was only made of skin-coloured clay.

A face is a man, a bald juryman cries,
for one face lost, another man dies.

Gentlemen, this citizen we daren't acquit
until we know what he did with it.

It was only a face, your honour, that I lost;
how much can such a sad thing cost?

A mask is a lifetime, my bad man,
to replace such a gift nobody can.

Consider the case of that jovial swan
who took a god's face off to put a bird's face on

and Leda swooning by the side of the sea
and the swan's eyes closed in lechery.

No! No! your honour, my aim was just –
I did what every true man must.

Quiet, prisoner! Why I remember a priest remark
that he picked up a dog's face in the dark,

then he got as drunk as a man can be
and barked at God in blasphemy.

But it was a human face, sir, I cast away;
for that offence do I have to pay?

The heads around the table disagree,
some say hang him from the gallows tree.

Some say high and some say low
to swing, swing, swing, when the free winds blow.

At the back of the courtroom quietly stand
his father and mother hand-in-hand.

They can't understand the point of this case
or why he discarded his own dear face.

But it's not *my* face, father, he had said,
I don't want to die in a strange, wrong bed.

Look in the mirror, mother, stare in deep;
is that mask your own, yours to keep?

The mirror is oblong, the clock is round,
all our wax faces go underground.

Once, I built a bridge right into myself
to ransack my soul for invisible wealth

and, afterwards, I tore off my mask because
I found not the person I thought I was.

With the wrong mask, another man's life I live –
I must seek my own face, find my own grave.

The heads around the table disagree,
some say hang him from the gallows tree.

Some say high and some say low
to swing, swing, swing, when the free winds blow.

I'll sum up, the severe Judge moans,
showing the white of his knucklebones.

What is a face but the thing that you see,
the symbol and fate of identity?

How would we recognize each from each:
a dog from a man – which face on a leash?

And when tears fall where no face is,
will the tears be mine or will they be his?

To select hot coal or gold no man is free,
each choice being determined by identity.

But exchange your face then what you choose
is gained, like love, by what you lose.

Now you twelve jurymen please retire,
put your right hands in ice and your left in fire.

A hole where the face was frightens us,
and a man who can choose is dangerous.

So what is your verdict going to be,
should he be hung from a gallows tree?

Oh some say high and some say low
to swing, swing, swing, when the free winds blow.

Verses at Night

Sleepless, by the windowpane I stare –
   black aeroplanes displace black air.
   The lazar moon glares down aghast.
      The seven branched tree is bare.

Oh how much like Europe's gothic Past!
   This scene my nightmare's protoplast:
   glow of the radioactive worm.
      Future story of the Blast?

Unreal? East and West fat Neros yearn
   for other fiddled Romes to burn;
   and so dogma cancels dogma
      and heretics in their turn.

By my wife now, I lie quiet as a
    thought of how moon and stars might blur,
    and miles of smoke squirm overhead
      rising to Man's arbiter;

the grey skin shrivelling from the head,
    our two skulls in the double bed,
    leukaemia in the soul of all
      flowing through the blood instead.

'No,' I shout, as by her side I sprawl,
    'No,' again, as I hear my small,
    dear daughter whimper in her cot
      and across the darkness call.

New Babylons

When psaltery and dulcimer
sound the King's musick,
the plebs kneel in homage
before the Golden Image.
Shadrach, Meshack, Abed-nego,
through the open furnace go,
three only and heroic.

The Court will not adjourn.
Time's fires leap and burn
and mavericks such as I
must be branded in their turn –
to reek of human flesh
whilst venal courtiers cry:
'Conform, conform or die.'

Still I'd shout out, 'No,'
like a Daniel condemned
to prove timeless honesties.
Let spellbound lions know
an angel in the den
lest they bite to please
the vast majorities.

Outside is a lonely place.
But within there's barely space
to embrace each other.
Edicts from the palace
as lover fumbles lover
and cynical voices cry:
'Conform, conform and die.'

Oh where is Daniel now?
Even tall rebels submit
to patterns of conformity.
I think of Babylon and admit
the hands of Time move on,
unpick us all, leave us in
uniforms of the skeleton.

Oppose, oppose, orthodoxies.
Though the furnace doors are shut,
small fires leap up high.
Cornet, drums, and sackbut,
could raise a tyrant's melodies
and the severe Judges cry:
'Conform, conform or die.'

So hearing in the Square
another maverick's despair,
as crowds draw near and shout
dark curses on the air,
where is the Daniel who
will not kneel in doubt
and will not turn about?

This, the Image of the Age:
police bring truncheons down
and each blow is our own.
When Nebuchadnezzars rage
no maverick is immune
for it's we, ourselves, who cry:
'Conform, conform and die.'

Emperors of the Island

A political parable to be read aloud

There is the story of a deserted island
where five men walked down to the bay.

The story of this island is
that three men would two men slay.

Three men dug two graves in the sand,
three men stood on the sea wet rock,
three shadows moved away.

There is the story of a deserted island
where three men walked down to the bay.

The story of this island is
that two men would one man slay.

Two men dug one grave in the sand,
two men stood on the sea wet rock,
two shadows moved away.

There is the story of a deserted island
where two men walked down to the bay.

The story of this island is
that one man would one man slay.

One man dug one grave in the sand,
one man stood on the sea wet rock,
one shadow moved away.

There is the story of a deserted island
where four ghosts walked down to the bay.

The story of this island is
that four ghosts would one man slay.

Four ghosts dug one grave in the sand,
four ghosts stood on the sea wet rock;
five ghosts moved away.

Social Revolution in England

Insolent as waiters, they did not ring the bell.
    Some slid down banisters, stomped up again.
    We assumed they were agencies from hell
    but why they had come no one was certain.
Best to smile like landlords, offer a jargonelle.

Number Thirteen, we said distracted, is next door.
    Often cold politeness works quite neatly.
    They brushed us aside trying to ignore
    our hints, the nice way we coughed discreetly.
They just ran up and down the staircase as before.

Preternatural bailiffs, they stripped the house bare
    of properties. Light the oblong patches
    on walls where once our gouty fathers were.
    We heard them talking in dirty snatches
as heavy doors opened. Our eyes began to blur.

It was as if we weren't, like phantoms, there at all
    and they in some intimate, cruel game
    engaged – horrid, olid, and medieval.
    Why ask why, from exactly where they came
when ergatocracies, too, in time must fall?

Who'd query such common, anonymous powers?
    By asking questions man becomes insane.
    In the empty hall now we've waited hours
    by the telephone for someone to explain,
to send some message, even if it's only flowers.

The Second Coming

The ground twitches and the noble head
(so often painted) breaks through the cracked crust,
hair first, then ivory forehead into the sunlit field;
the earth yields silently to the straining.
A blackbird flies away.

The eyes open suddenly
just above the grass, seeing corn. No man is near.
Sound of days of heat, of silence.
It is lonely to be born.
And now he's breathing – air not earth
who inhaled worms and death so long.

Still his body in darkness, lightward pushing.
Pause, rest, he is tired now, enough to delight
in looking. Is this true: the world all heaven,
head in corn, with pale butterflies
staggering over him?

He cannot rise further.
The earth is heavy on his shoulders.
Cry out, shout, oh help is near.
Dangerously, the machine passes scything corn,
but the driver does not hear, cannot hear
– and now that noble head is gone,
a liquid redness in the yellow
where the mouth had been.

Dig, I say dig, you'll
find arms, loins, white legs, to prove my story –
and one red poppy in the corn.

Looking at a Map

The map does not show the rain:
only pale blue for sea and Great Britain
a mosaic of multi-coloured counties
where the English weather never changes,
and the local hills and mountain ranges
are shaded heavily – though never white
   as moods of snow may shade them.

   Clouds never shamble over
unless this cigarette-smoke I blow out
be cloud; this sad electric bulb be sun
where constellations of flies (not planets)
   all silently swing about.

   False! False! Boring lines squiggle,
meaning empty roads, hedges and wet tyres;
or desolation of damp railway lines
where no one encounters a red lamp danger.
   But there's menace of a kind.
Why else do official cartographers
   condemn the whole land behind
a strict cage emptied of noughts and crosses
where no happy latitude is given?

And this, too, another lie:
this measurement of a lifetime's journey
in inches, these little, exact circles
for names of places where untamed people
    privately hide and love and cry.

Enough, I switch off the electric bulb,
    the thin current of the sun.
Oh nightly, something secret breathes and moves;
    the whole flat, civilized map
that here is cracked into coloured counties,
    like energy explodes, goes black;
    these names of cities break out
into dotty, shifting points of glitterings,
    and the light blue tide flows back.

Elegy for Dylan Thomas

    All down the valleys they are talking,
    and in the community of the smoke-laden town.
Tomorrow, through bird-trailed skies, across labouring
    waves,
wrong-again Emily will come to the dandelion yard
    and, with rum tourists, inspect his grave.

Death was his voluntary marriage,
and his poor silence sold to that rich and famous bride.
   Beleaguered in that essential kiss he rode
the whiskey-meadows of her breath till, mortal, voiceless,
   he gave up his nailed ghost and he died.

   No more to celebrate
his disinherited innocence or your half-buried heart
      drunk as a butterfly, or sober as black.
Now, one second from earth, not even for the sake
      of love can his true energy come back.

   So cease your talking.
Too familiar you blaspheme his name and collected legends:
   some tears fall soundlessly and aren't the same
      as those that drop with obituary explosions.
      Suddenly, others who sing seem older and lame.

   But far from the blind country of prose,
wherever his burst voice goes about you or through you,
   look up in surprise, in a hurt public house
      or in a rain-blown street, and see how
      no fat ghost but a quotation cries.

   Stranger, he is laid to rest
not in the nightingale dark nor in the canary light.
   At the dear last, the yolk broke in his head,
   blood of his soul's egg in a splash of bright
      voices and now he is dead.

December, 1953

Enter The Movement

They said proudly, 'Our demon', pointing to
the Boat-house and the famous tenant who
sang in the night with half the lights put out.
Sometimes his song was true, no mere ranting shout.

Sensual intruders rejoiced and danced
to his gorgeous music and, if in time, it chanced
the ceiling sagged with sound and the walls cracked,
well, he sang the Welsh passion others lacked.

His powerful voice broke all the windows,
which transparencies must be paid in prose
not by wild fictions of a singing clown.
Some applauded when his roof fell down.

Then winter came when whistling beggars freeze.
He, to quench inner fires, drank catastrophes
while corybants, roaring, jigged with joy outside
till, delirious, that lyric singer died.

Now all cry, 'Regard that desperate ruin
of a life, example of Dionysian sin,'
and begin to rebuild, replace the roof,
finding one devil damnable enough.

The new choir that moves in is neat and sane
and dare not whistle in the dark again.
Proudly English, they sing with sharp, flat voices
but no-one dances, nobody rejoices.

The Moment

You raise your eyes from the level book
as if deeply listening. You are further than I call.
Like Eurydice you wear a hurt and absent look,
but I'm gentle for the silence into which you fall so sadly.
What are you thinking? Do you love me?
Suddenly you are not you at all but a ghost
dreaming of a castle to haunt or a heavy garden;
some place eerie, and far from me. But now a door
is banging outside, so you turn your head surprised.

You speak my name and someone else has died.

Poem and Message

Out on the tormented, midnight sea
your sails are blown in jeopardy.
Gales of grief and terrors force
you from the spirit's chartered course.

But, in the storm, lighthouses mark
rocks of dangers in the dark;
so from this shore of cold I write
tiny flashes in the night.

Words of safety, words of love,
a beacon in the dark to save
you from the catastrophic sea,
and navigate you home to me.

Dear, vague as a distant star, I,
in the huge night's amorphous lie,
find one small and luminous truth
of which our usual love was proof.

And I call your name as loud I can
and give you all the light I am.

Anniversary

(On Primrose Hill)

The tree grows down from a bird.
The strong grass pulls up the earth
to a hill. Wade here, my dear,
through green shallows of daisies.
I hear the voice talking that is dead
behind the voice that is talking now.
The clocks of the smoky town
strike a quiet, grating sound.
Tomorrow will be the same.
Two sit on this hill and count
two moving from the two that stayed.

What happens to a flame blown out?
What perishes? Not this view
with my magnified hand in yours
whatever hurt and angers done.
I breathe in air the dead breathed out.
When first you inclined your face
to mine, my sweet ally came,
with your brown eyes purely wide.
My right hand on your left breast
I said, I have little to tell my dear.
For the pure bird, a pure cage.

Oh the silence that you lost
in the pandemonium
of the kiss and ruined was.
My dear, my dear, what perishes?
I hear this voice in a voice to come.

Poem of Celebration

I lean against the air.
It gives way like unstitched water. I fall in
but am drowned in air. Now distinctly
every image reflects the invisible world.

The noise divides from the light.
Bold astronomers who at night
peep through the windowpane of the colossal skies
look too far for the furthest star.
This world confirms my senses.

Swaying and drunk with seeing
the near magnificence of things,
I cry out a doxology with the surprise
of a shout, creating maximum silence.

How else may I give thanks, give praise,
but to trap a visible poem
in the invisible cage and leave it there?
Look, I'm back again to where you are.
I came through a hole in the air.

Enriched forever. Hardly evangelical
but still my rainbowed heart blessed and thumping.
Any man may gather the images of despair;
I'll say 'I will' and 'I can'
and like an accident breathe in space and air.

The Victim of Aulis

A multitude of masts in the harbour.
The sails limp in the air, becalmed.
The tired sea barely moving.
   The sea breathes quietly, Agamemnon.
      The wind is dead.
The sunlight leaping the waters,
the waters lapping at the boats.
Heat haze.
The King prowls the still deck
back and fore while the Captains quarrel.
We only throw dice and curse.
   The child! The child!
The whisper of the sea, the secret of the sea;
the sea is dreaming and a tall slave sings.
   What are we to do?
      They will think of a way.
         We have had nothing of education
            We must obey, being little men.
         The cause is just.
            Leave it to the Captains.
               What does Calchas say?
                  The child! The child!
And we thinking of our own daughters
with clumsy father-pride,
though those other virgins are faceless now
indistinct as the mingling of voices,
as the shuffle of the sea,
the little sound of the sea.
   It has been a long time.
      Leave it to the priests.
Conference at Aulis.

And he, the King, listening to the whisper of Calchas,
to the sea restless in its sleep while a tall slave sings –
sings of home and alien distances,
a slow voice, sad as a light,
as a flame burning in daytime.
   Agamemnon is in religion.
      It's that or nothing now.
         The child! The child!
And she peering down through the fathomless minds
of the sea, at green shadows and dark dreams of fish –
for the deep thoughts of the sea are fish –
and she trailing her small hands in the waters
playing with coloured beads of spray.
   Come with me.
      Why father?
We sit on the stone quay with the sun and the seagulls.
   We know nothing of rough mythologies, only
         facts.
   We need the gods more than they need us.
         And never again will some come home,
Artemis is offended, Calchas said,
staring at golden bangles spinning on the sea,
at arrows of poisoned sunlight pricking the flat sea;
the yellow masts vertical, pointing at the blue, luxurious sky,
the white sails lagging down, without life, without wind.
Calchas mumbles: Troy, Troy.
We only throw dice and curse the dawn we sailed away,
grumble and tell lewd tales of faithless women,
remembering Helen ravished in a foreign bed.
   The child! The child!
And the King musing: what will her mother say?

The sigh and the sadness of it. And she who has no breasts
trailing her small hands in the waters, just a child,
still a child – that is a fearful thing.
    Come with me.
        Why father?
Murder at Aulis.
Oh the questions of the young-to-be-slain,
and the memory of black eyelashes pulled apart suddenly
revealing more white of the eye than a man bargained for.
The King is in religion
whose name is great among the Greeks –
the blood, ridiculously crimson in the groves of Artemis,
and the wind howling, why father? why father?
for many days and louder in the silence of the night,
and distressing him and possessing him in the mornings,
in the sea-spray climbing, and in the sea-howl,
as the fleet drags on aslant in the furious wind.
They thought of a way.
We are little men
who follow and obey
as the cracked sails billow out half below the leaping sea,
as the tall slave sings why Father? why Father?

The Game

Follow the crowds to where the turnstiles click.
The terraces fill. *Hoompa*, blares the brassy band.
Saturday afternoon has come to Ninian Park
and, beyond the goal posts, in the Canton Stand
between black spaces, a hundred matches spark.

Waiting, we recall records, legendary scores:
Fred Keenor, Hardy, in a royal blue shirt.
The very names, sad as the old songs, open doors
before our time where someone else was hurt.
Now, like an injured beast, the great crowd roars.

The coin is spun. Here all is simplified,
and we are partisan who cheer the Good,
hiss at passing Evil. Was Lucifer offside?
A wing falls down when cherubs howl for blood.
Demons have agents: the Referee is bribed.

The white ball smacked the crossbar. Satan rose
higher than the others in the smoked brown gloom
to sink on grass in a ballet dancer's pose.
Again it seems we hear a familiar tune
not quite identifiable. A distant whistle blows.

Memory of faded games, the discarded years;
talk of Aston Villa, Orient, and the Swans.
Half-time, the band played the same military airs
as when the Bluebirds once were champions.
Round touchlines the same cripples in their chairs.

Mephistopheles had his joke. The honest team
dribbles ineffectively, no one can be blamed.
Infernal backs tackle, inside forwards scheme,
and if they foul us need we be ashamed?
Heads up! Oh for a Ted Drake, a Dixie Dean.

'Saved' or else, discontents, we are transferred
long decades back, like Faust must pay that fee.
The night is early. Great phantoms in us stir
as coloured jerseys hover, move diagonally
on the damp turf, and our eidetic visions blur.

God sign our souls! Because the obscure staff
of Hell rule this world, jugular fans guessed
the result halfway through the second half,
and those who know the score just seem depressed.
Small boys swarm the field for an autograph.

Silent the stadium. The crowds have all filed out.
Only the pigeons beneath the roofs remain.
The clean programmes are trampled underfoot,
and natural the dark, appropriate the rain,
whilst, under lamp-posts, threatening newsboys shout.

The Race

We three crouched down ready to go,
Past, Present and Future. Although
the race was rigged, we didn't know.

Now, my head low in shy disgrace,
I move into the second place
and try to hold this killing pace

and gain my second breath. I curse,
seeing the countryside in reverse:
the road slide back to where I was.

I feel my formed face change. And run
yet faster to let Thy Will be done.
Look, I spurt towards Kingdom Come.

Behind me I hear the Present shout:
'Why don't they jeer and carry me out;
what is the silence all about?'

The old dream I carry on my back
is the chaos the other two lack.
I sprint to the inside of the track.

Drawing near I hear the Future cry,
'I am your death and prophecy,
but in transforming you I die.'

Just in front that champion lies.
Our four legs together harmonize
till I pass him for the final prize.

In the stadium the brash crowd roar.
I know what they are calling for;
but will my fading dream endure?

Here is the Hangman and the Tree,
shapes of some green allegory;
I run towards the world to be.

Now I'm the Future who was the Past,
at last I lead who once was last.
I round another lap, sprinting fast.

Ahead I see the winning post.
I finish first and so have lost
and speed into my walking ghost.

Tyrant

Tyrant of every Court,
voice shaking the silence,
not for long can happiness
transport us from your claim
whose subjects must obey.
As gongs announce your fame
we're back in time again.

World makes love go round
but the lover always falls
when the other moves away
and well inside Time's walls.
Dreams' insanities may
muffle your sounds of sound,
deny all your numerals.

But by extracting green
that Court is overcome.
Undress, love, roll back the scene,
view jubilantly the One
O metamorphosis
till we in grace are dumb,
and religious as a kiss.

But Time's holiday must close.
A click, a whirr, a strike
and we return to prose.
Rings of an ancient bark
become as visible as
a phosphorescent watch
and numbers in the dark.

Stars, stars, lengths of light
and though they swerve and fade
while rude the cockerels crow,
our skins are cruelly timed:
the filth begins to show.
Grave men dig their spades
to grate on bones below.

44

All are condemned to Death.
How, knowing, can we live?
For ignorance of Time
is the blest prerogative
of consuming animals,
merciless and divine.
Our escapes are tentative.

Murderer and Master,
all your frontiers close.
Only the Dead elope.
Bells, bells, rock out faithlight
as towards the dark we grope.
Tick, tick, here's the trapdoor.
Tock. There's the rope.

1954, 2002

Public Library

Who, in the public library, one evening after rain,
amongst the polished tables and linoleum,
stands bored under blank light to glance at these pages?
Whose absent mood, like neon glowing in the night,
is conversant with wet pavements, nothing to do?

Neutral, the clock-watching girl stamps out the date,
a forced celebration, a posthumous birthday,
her head buttered by the drizzling library lamps;
yet the accident of words, too, can light the semi-dark
should the reader lead them home, generously journey,
later to return, perhaps leaving a bus ticket as a bookmark.

Who wrote in margins hieroglyphic notations,
that obscenity, deleted this imperfect line?
Read by whose hostile eyes, in what bed-sitting rooms,
in which rainy, dejected railway stations?

The Water Diviner

Late, I have come to a parched land
doubting my gift, if gift I have,
the inspiration of water
spilt, swallowed by the sand.

To hear once more water trickle,
to stand in a stretch of silence
the divining pen twisting in the hand:
sign of depths alluvial.

Water owns no permanent shape,
sags, is most itself in chaos;
now, under the shadow of the idol,
dry mouth and dry landscape.

No rain falls with a refreshing sound
to settle tubular in a well,
elliptical in a bowl. No grape
lusciously moulds it round.

Clouds have no constant resemblance
to anything, blown by a hot wind,
flying mirages; the blue background,
light constructions of chance.

To hold back chaos I transformed
amorphous mass: clay, fire, or cloud,
so that the agèd gods might dance
and golden structures form.

I should have built, plain brick on brick,
a water tower. The sun flies on
arid wastes, barren hells too warm
and me with a hazel stick!

Rivulets vanished in the dust
long ago, great compositions
vaporized, salt on the tongue so thick
that drinking still I thirst.

Repeated desert, recurring drought,
sometimes hearing water trickle,
sometimes not, I, by doubting first,
believe: believing, doubt.

Return to Cardiff

'Hometown'; well, most admit an affection for a city:
grey, tangled streets I cycled on to school, my first cigarette
in the back lane, and, fool, my first botched love affair.
First everything. Faded torments; self-indulgent pity.

The journey to Cardiff seemed less a return than a raid
on mislaid identities. Of course the whole locus smaller:
the mile-wide Taff now a stream, the castle not as in some
    black,
gothic dream, but a decent sprawl, a joker's toy façade.

Unfocused voices in the wind, associations, clues,
odds and ends, fringes caught, as when, after the doctor quit,
a door opened and I glimpsed the white, enormous face
of my grandfather, suddenly aghast with certain news.

Unable to define anything I can hardly speak,
and still I love the place for what I wanted it to be
as much as for what it unashamedly is
now for me, a city of strangers, alien and bleak.

Unable to communicate I'm easily betrayed,
uneasily diverted by mere sense reflections
like those anchored waterscapes that wander, alter, in the
    Taff,
hour by hour, as light slants down a different shade.

Illusory, too, that lost dark playground after rain,
the noise of trams, gunshots in what they once called Tiger
    Bay.
Only real this smell of ripe, damp earth when the sun comes
    out,
a mixture of pungencies, half exquisite and half plain.

No sooner than I'd arrived the other Cardiff had gone,
smoke in the memory, these but tinned resemblances,
where the boy I was not and the man I am not
met, hesitated, left double footsteps, then walked on.

Summer's Sunday Song

At this village, religious as a psalm,
    peaceful by this English river's edge,
light visits the undersides of bridges,
    midges dare the olive waters calm.
        Come prepare yourself, disarm.

Where punt, and willow tree, and swan contend
    for mastery of the humbled eye,
even Ophelia could come floating by
    consoled. Inaudible organs sound.
        Now advance on lyric ground.

Late, the sun clings on biscuit-coloured walls
     of mellowed farmhouse, hallowed chapel.
Smoked gold shafts ignite high branches, dapple
     the woods with shadows. This path compels.
          Green vibrating fields like bells.

Grave nature, how the pious dark is pale,
     trippers in the gloom restart their cars.
Let the ear (thatched roofs sag below the stars)
     usurp the eye: owl and nightingale
          orchestrate your holy tale.

Sunday Evening

Loved not for themselves those tenors who sing
arias from 'Aida' on horned, tinny
gramophones – but because they take a man back
to a half forgotten thing.

We, transported by this evening loaded
with a song recorded by Caruso,
recall some other place, another time,
now charmingly outmoded.

What, for wrong motives, too often is approved
proves we once existed, becomes mere flattery
– then it's ourselves whom we are listening to,
and, by hearing, we are moved.

To know, haunted, this echo too will fade
with fresh alliteration of the leaves,
as more rain, indistinct, drags down the sky
like a sense of gloom mislaid.

Dear classic, melodic absences
how stringently debarred, kept out of mind,
till some genius on a gramophone
holes defences, breaks all fences.

What lives in a man and calls him back
and back through desolate Sunday evenings?
Indescribable, oh faint generic name:
sweet taste, bitter lack.

The Magician

Off stage, the Great Illusionist owns bad teeth,
cheats at cards, beats his second wife, is lewd;
before studying his art he qualified
as obsessional liar, petty thief.

Transformed by glamorous paraphernalia –
tall top hat, made-up face, four smoking spotlights –
only fellow magicians can sense beneath
that glossy surface a human failure.

Ready with unseen wires, luminous paint,
with drums and ceremony he fills the stage,
rich twice nightly in his full regalia.
Two extras planted in the audience faint.

Allezup! Closes his eyes, seemingly bored,
and astutely fakes a vulgar miracle,
mutters and reclines to become fakir, saint;
on a hotbed of nails, swallows a sword.

For encore will saw a seedy blonde in half
as music rises to a shrill crescendo;
hacks through wood, skin, vertebrae, spinal cord,
and all except the gods applaud or laugh.

Lord, red blood oozes from the long black box,
oh hocus pocus, oh abracadabra,
whilst, in trumped-up panic, manager and staff
race breathlessly on stage, undo the locks.

Patrons prefer bisected blondes to disappear.
Relieved, commercial men and their average wives
now salaciously prepare for further shocks,
eagerly yearn to see what they most fear.

Sometimes, something he cannot understand
happens – atavistic powers stray unleashed,
a raving voice he hardly thought to hear,
the ventriloquist's dummy out of hand.

In the box, a vision of himself – and on
those masochistic nails fresh genuine blood,
within his white glove a decomposing hand,
and, unimaginably, his own face gone.

Quite disturbed the disconnected audience boo.
What cheek! This charlatan believes his magic:
not luminous paint across the darkness shone
when, happily, for once, his lies came true.

Or so it seemed. Oh what overbearing pride
if no longer fake but Great Illusionist;
but as phoney critics pierce him through and through
he begs for mercy and is justified.

Off stage, that Great Illusionist owns bad teeth,
cheats at cards, beats his second wife, is lewd;
before studying his art he qualified
as obsessional liar, petty thief.

The French Master

Everyone in Class II at the Grammar School
had heard of Walter Bird, known as Wazo.
They said he'd behead each dullard and fool
or, instead, carve off a tail for the fun.

Wazo's cane buzzed like a bee in the air.
Quietly, quietly, in the desks of Form III
sneaky Wazo tweaked our ears and our hair.
Walter Wazo, public enemy No. 1.

Five feet tall, he married sweet Doreen Wall,
and combmarks furrowed his vaselined hair;
his hands still fluttered ridiculously small,
his eyes the colour of a poison bottle.

Who'd think he'd falter, poor love-sick Walter
as bored he read out *Lettres de mon Moulin*;
his mouth had begun to soften and alter,
and Class IV ribbed him as only boys can.

Perhaps through kissing his wife to a moan
had alone changed the shape of his lips,
till the habit of her mouth became his own:
no more Walter Wazo, enemy No. 1.

'Boy', he'd whine, 'yes, please decline the verb to have,'
in tones dulcet and mild as a girl.
'Sorry sir, can't sir, must go to the lav,'
whilst Wazo stared out of this world.

Till one day in May Wazo buzzed like a bee
and stung, twice, many a warm, inky hand;
he stormed through the form, a catastrophe,
returned to this world, No. 1.

Alas, alas, to the Vth Form's disgrace
nobody could quote Villon to that villain.
Again the nasty old mouth zipped on his face,
and not a weak-bladdered boy in the class.

Was Doreen being kissed by a Mr Anon?
Years later, I purred, 'Your dear wife, Mr Bird?'
Teeth bared, how he *glared* before stamping on;
and suddenly I felt sorry for the bastard.

The Abandoned

There is no space unoccupied by the Shekinah. Talmud

. . . thy absence doth excel
All distance known. George Herbert

I

God, when you came to our house
   we let you in. Hunted,
      we gave you succour,
         bandaged your hands,
            bathed your feet.

Wanting water we gave you wine.
Wanting bread we gave you meat.

Sometimes, God, you should recall
    we are your hiding-place.
        Take away these hands
            and you would fall.

Outside, the afflicted pass.
    We only have to call.
        They would open you
            with crutch and glass.

Who else then could we betray
    if not you, the nearest?
        God, how you watch us
            and shrink away.

2

Never have we known you so transparent.
You stand against the curtain and wear
its exact design. And if a window opens
(like a sign) then is it you
or the colours that are blown apart?

You startle from room to room, apologizing.

God, you can't help your presence
any more than the glassy air that lies
between tree and skies. No need to pass
through wavelengths human ears can't sense.

We never hear the front door close when you are leaving.
Sometimes we question if you are there at all.
No need to be so self-effacing;
quiet as language of the roses
or moss upon a wall.

We have to hold our breath to hear you breathing.

3

Dear God in the end you had to go.
Dismissing you, your absence made us sane.
We keep the bread and wine for show.

The white horse galloped across the snow,
melted, leaving no hoofmarks in the rain.
Dear God, in the end you had to go.

The winds of war and derelictions blow,
howling across the radioactive plain.
We keep the bread and wine for show.

Sometimes what we do not know we know –
who can count the stars, call each one by name?
Dear God in the end you had to go.

Yet boarding the last ship out we sorrow
that grape is but grape and grain is grain.
We keep the bread and wine for show.

Soon night will be like feathers of the crow,
small lights upon the shore begin to wane.
Dear God in the end you had to go.
We keep the bread and wine for show.

4

Now, God, you are the colour black.
Who prays, 'Come down, thou, come down?'
Absurd saints search for the rack.
Plumed Popes begin to doubt, lose track.
'Did the shadow answer back?'

It was their own voice, God, that cried.
So who slammed shut the bolt
against the human noise outside?
Oh open the damned door wide.
Maybe someone dear has died.

Listen. Can't you hear again
an idiot desperate in a house,
the strict economy of pain,
a voice pleading and profane
calling you by name?

1957, 2001

Tree

Grotesquely shaped, this stubbed tree craves a madman's eye,
its convoluted pipes lie tortured on the air,
twist black, turn back to fanged twigs and attitudes,
its dusty leaves quite stunted, still it will not die.

In rousing spring its frugal green was last to bud,
in autumn will be the first to anticipate the fall.
Now, aimlessly, I give it human attributes:
its mud-coloured bark, sick flesh; sap, a victim's blood.

As, sometimes, a child, contorting his plastic face
to make another laugh, is told to cease his play
lest abstract fate solidifies both lips and eyes,
horrifically, to one perpetual grimace;

so, perhaps, this maimed structure postured once and thus –
a buffoon amidst these oaks. Then laughter shook
untimely leaves down till avenging lightning struck,
petrified the attitude, a spectacle for us.

August – other trees conform, are properly dressed;
but this funny one exists for funny children,
easy to climb, easy to insult, or throw stones at,
and only urgent lovers in its shade will rest.

Yet this pauper, this caliban tree, let good men praise,
for it survives, and that's enough; more, on gala nights,
with copper beech and silver birch it too can soar
unanchored, free, in prosperous moonlight and amaze.

Odd

In front of our house in Golders Green
the lawn, like a cliché, mutters, 'Rose bushes.'
The whole suburb is very respectable.
Ugly men drive past in funeral suits,
from their necks you can tell they're overweight.

Sodium lamp-posts, at night, hose empty roads
with gold which treacles over pavement trees,
polishes brittle hedges, clings on closed, parked cars.
If a light should fly on in an upstairs room
odds on two someones are going to sleep.

It's unusual to meet a beggar,
you hardly ever see a someone drunk.
It's a nice, clean, quiet, religious place.
For my part, now and then, I want to scream:
thus, by the neighbours, am considered odd.

From the sensible wastes of Golders Green
I journey to Soho where a job owns me.
Soho is not a respectable place.
Underweight women in the gamiest of skirts
bleed a smile of false teeth at ugly men.

Later, the dark is shabby with paste electric
of peeporamas, brothels, clubs and pubs,
restaurants that sport sallow waiters who cough.
If a light should fly on in an upstairs room
odds on two someones are going to bed.

It's customary to see many beggars,
common to meet people roaring and drunk.
It's a nice, loud, dirty, irreligious place.
For my part, now and then, I want to scream:
thus, by Soho friends, am considered odd.

After the Release of Ezra Pound

In Jerusalem I asked
the ancient Hebrew poets to forgive you,
and what would Walt Whitman have said
and Thomas Jefferson?   Paul Potts

In Soho's square mile of unoriginal sin
where the fraudulent neon lights haunt,
but cannot hide, the dinginess of vice,
the jeans and sweater boys spoke of Pound,
and you, Paul, repeated your question.

The chee-chee bums in Torino's laughed and
the virgins of St Martin's School of Art.
The corner spivs with their Maltese masks
loitered for the two o'clock result,
and those in the restaurants of Greek Street,
eating income tax, did not hear the laugh.

Gentle Gentile, you asked the question.
Free now (and we praise this) Pound could answer.

The strip lighting of Soho did not fuse,
no blood trickled from a certain book
down the immaculate shelves of Zwemmer's.
But the circumcised did not laugh.
The swart nudes in the backrooms put on clothes
and the doors of the French pub closed.

Pound did not hear the raw Jewish cry,
the populations committed to the dark
when he muttered through the microphones
of murderers. He, not I, must answer.

Because of the structures of a beautiful poet
you ask the man who is less than beautiful,
and wait in the public neurosis of Soho,
in the liberty of loneliness for an answer.

In the beer and espresso bars they talked
of Ezra Pound, excusing the silences of an old man,
saying there is so little time between
the parquet floors of an institution
and the boredom of the final box.

Why, Paul, if that ticking distance between
was merely a journey long enough
to walk the circumference of a Belsen,
Walt Whitman would have been eloquent,
and Thomas Jefferson would have cursed.

Spring, 1958

Red Balloon

It sailed across the startled town,
over chapels, over chimney-pots,
wind-blown above a block of flats
before it floated down.

Oddly, it landed where I stood,
and finding's keeping, as you know.
I breathed on it, I polished it,
till it shone like living blood.

It was my shame, it was my joy,
it brought me notoriety.
From all of Wales the rude boys came,
it ceased to be a toy.

I heard the girls of Cardiff sigh
when my balloon, my red balloon,
soared higher like a happiness
towards the dark blue sky.

Nine months since, have I boasted of
my unique, my only precious;
but to no one dare I show it now
however long they swear their love.

'It's a Jew's balloon,' my best friend cried,
'stained with our dear Lord's blood.'
'That I'm a Jew is true,' I said,
said I, 'that cannot be denied.'

'What relevance?' I asked, surprised,
'what's religion to do with this?'
'Your red balloon's a Jew's balloon,
let's get it circumcised.'

Then some boys laughed and some boys cursed,
some unsheathed their dirty knives;
some lunged, some clawed at my balloon,
but still it would not burst.

They bled my nose, they cut my eye,
half conscious in the street I heard,
'Give up, give up your red balloon.'
I don't know exactly why.

Father, bolt the door, turn the key,
lest those sad, brash boys return
to insult my faith and steal
my red balloon from me.

Postmark

Envelopes that come with an official stamp,
to conjure up visions of IN and OUT trays,
make me think of death, of Jewish funerals,
lost afternoons faded and damp.

Of course it's a private association.
Other happenings may signify – maybe
a picture frame that falls down, suddenly, prompts
you to morbid speculation.

Anyway, the dead were alien as could be,
fit for red tape, odd names on a *proforma*;
even their relatives gathering had little,
if anything, to do with me.

Till one laundry-coloured, sky-blown day,
    a telegram –
then a phone clamouring in a quiet hall
immured a familiar though stylized voice:
synagogue doors began to slam.

Pecking typewriters were hushed, an unseen staff
filed in and out subdued, put slang in a drawer,
as I whispered above the wail of Hebrew
so shocked that I wanted to laugh.

Yet I inhabited a serious suit;
black tie, an uncreased face to match;
observed dust in sunbeams whilst knowing uncles
washed dry hands, appeared astute,

owned an awkward correctness as can be found
in civic buildings (whose linoleum smell
wafts along corridors to offices where,
on Sundays, there is not a sound).

Though a mere youth I'd heard about this pogrom
or that – and thought, whether in York or in Dachau,
Death had something to do with the Government.
Nobody told me I was wrong.

I don't know why else an official postmark
should make me think thus. He whom I mourned is
half forgot: a sandpaper chin, a smile, a voice,
and the rest is not silence but dark.

The Grand View

Mystics, in their far, erotic stance,
neglect our vulgar catastrophes.
I, with cadence, rhyme and assonance,
must pardon their oceanic trance,
their too saintlike immoralities.

For I, too, spellbound by the grand view,
flung through vistas from this windy hill,
am in pure love. I do not know who
it is that I love, but I would flow
into One invisible and still.

Though islanded and inspired by
the merely human, I sing back robes of air
to uncover my ego-plundered eye,
abandoning my apostasy,
no more to make a home out of despair.

Only Moses on the high mountain
at least knew what he was climbing for.
God-haunted, wonderstruck, half insane,
that condemned genius brought down again
ten social poems we call the law.

My littleness makes but a private sound,
the little lyric of a little man;
yet, like Moses, I walk on holy ground
since all earth is, and the world is round
I come back to where he began.

My forehead is open. The horns grow out
and exit. Infirm cynics knock inside,
and still ancestral voices shout
visions, visions! Should I turn about
if, by naming all, One is denied?

There are moments when a man must sing
of a lone Presence he cannot see.
To undulations of space I bring
all my love when love is happening;
green directions flying back to me.

There are moments when a man must praise
the astonishment of being alive,
when small mirrors of reality blaze
into miracles; and there's One always
who, by never departing, almost arrives.

Sunsets

I

This scene too beautiful it seems a fake,
these unlikely colours, this sky, that lake.
I have to close my eyes to keep awake.

Were all such lucid colours moving greys,
God's formal barbarities would amaze.
There is nothing else I may do but praise.

But speaking, I move into a future tense
to gain mere words, and lose the quiet sense
of wonder, destroying the experience.

Sunsets only exist that I may write
about them! Yet I'd dip my pen in light:
white print obscurely on a page of white.

2

Darkness, like terror, lies within the scene.
Music of Mozart merely seems serene.
He gazed at green till he became the green.

Mystics to keep awake close their eyes,
and, in eternal emptiness, feel wise.
God is what that great nothing signifies.

Oh the beautiful eyes of St Lucy
who plucked them out that she might see.
Such was her devotion to the Mystery.

The distance between two stars is night.
I stare and stare at dark till dark is bright.
Must I first go blind to have second sight?

3

Above that painted lake (of course unsigned)
its surface hoofed by colours in the wind,
there were windows between clouds and fires behind.

Light that irradiates is never dead,
so that violent heaven now lies in the head
and agonies of sky grow dark instead.

Past midnight, I re-create that gorgeous air
of sunset, its adorations of despair.
I stared at colour till I was the stare.

But since I can't breathe always with the five
senses naked, I wait for sleep to arrive,
and close both my eyes to keep alive.

Surprise! Surprise!

Talk not of loneliness, but aloneness.
Every thing is alien, everyone strange.
Regard an object closely, our own foot
named, how queer it appears as its toes flex.
Peer at it with greenhorn observation;
thus magnified, what incongruous toenails!
Or the tree outside, we pass every day,
stand below it, stare at it flagrantly
till it becomes uncomfortable, till
its slender boughs, shyly naked beneath
those veined, pellucid leaves, stir a little.
Scrutinized, it grows unrecognizable.
Again, utterly estranged, our colleague
who talks to us on weekdays – just the way
he walks, what a peculiar, indolent
manner of walking, come to think of it;
and lastly, that woman we love fondly,
sounded and labelled, who loves us perhaps,
look how she, while reading the newspaper,
taps her own forehead, checks her cheek, cheekbone,
nose, her martial lip, over and over,
withdrawn in concentration, unaware,

yet feels her face to affirm it's still there.
How then can we whisper, at night, 'My own'?
Oh how everything and everybody
are perplexed and perplexing, deeply unknown.
What surprises is that sometimes we are
not surprised, that a door clicks, half opens,
and we guessed beforehand who would enter.
Is that why we dare to cry: 'I know Smith'?
Now, which of you, suggesting I raise my head
from this page, will call my name familiarly?
You will see, as always, my eyes startled.

Two Voices

1   *A woman to a man*

To own nothing, but to be –
like the vagrant wind that bears
faintest fragrance of the sea
or, in anger, lifts and tears
yet hoards no property;

I praise that state of mind:
wind, music, and you, are such.
All the visible you find
(the invisible you touch)
alter, and leave behind.

To pure being you devote
all your days. You are your eyes,
seemingly near but remote.
Gone, now, the sense of surprise,
like a dying musical note.

Like fragrance, you left no trace,
like anger, you came my way,
like music, you filled the space
(by going, the more you stay).
Departures were in your face.

2   *A wife to a husband*

Doth the music always flee?
Who kiss, that they may own,
sing happily, oh happily
of brick on brick till stone
keeps out both wind and sea.

So come back fast, come back slow,
I'll be distance and your home,
every symbol that I know,
church, tower, mosque, and dome,
then by staying, the more you'll go.

Let me breath in music where
I am nothing but your life;
your designs, directions share,
to be no mistress but a wife,
pluck your meanings from the air.

I'll be all things you would be,
the four winds and the seven seas,
you'll play with such a gaiety
devastating melodies
till music be my body.

After a Departure

Intimate god of stations,
on long, faded afternoons
before impatient trains depart,
where the aching lovers wait
and mothers embarrass sons,
discover your natural art;
delicately articulate
an elegy of the heart
for horizons appropriate,
or dialogues for the stage
and the opening of an eye.

Love invents the sadness of
tolerable departures.
So bless every fumbling kiss
when eyes, hands, lips, betray
shy, tentative disclosures,
conclusions that non-lovers miss.
Taxis, buses, surge away
through the grey metropolis
while mortals frown for words to say,
and their ordinary messages
approximate, therefore lie.

Those heroes who departed
spouting famous monologues
were more verbose than we.
Antony at Paddington,
bizarre in his Roman togs,
a sword clanking on his knee,
would have jabbered on and on
love epithets most happily,
well after the train had gone.
Let prosy travellers rage
as long as Cleopatras sigh.

Romeo's peroration
for Juliet at Waterloo,
as gulps of steam arise
from the engine on its bit,
and from station-masters too,
would bring tears to the eyes.
Sooty god of stations permit
your express to dally, revise
timetables, dull schedules if it
allows one more classic page
or a Juliet to cry.

Today, I, your professional
pleb of words who must appear
spontaneous, who knows form
to be decorative logic,
whose style is in the error,
ask forgiveness for my storm
of silence when all speech grew sick;
who, waving from the platform,
found even gesture ironic,
afraid of your beautiful coinage
'I love you' and 'Goodbye'.

From a Suburban Window

Such afternoon glooms, such clouds chimney low –
London, the clouds want to move but can not,
London, the clouds want to rain but can not –
such negatives of a featureless day;
the street empty but for a van passing,
an afternoon smudged by old afternoons.
Soon, despite railings, evening will come
from a great distance trailing evenings.
Meantime, unemployed sadness loiters here.

Quite suddenly, six mourners appear:
a couple together, then three stout men,
then one more, lagging behind, bare-headed.
Not one of the six looks up at the sky,
and not one of them touches the railings.
They walk on and on remembering days,
yet seem content. They employ the décor.
They use this grey inch of eternity,
and the afternoon, so praised, grows distinct.

Close Up

Often you seem to be listening to a music
that others cannot hear. Rilke would have loved you:
you never intrude, you never ask questions
of those, crying in the dark, who are most near.

You always keep something of yourself to yourself
in the electric bars, even in bedrooms.
Rilke would have praised you: your nearness is far,
and, therefore, your distance like the very stars.

Yet some things you miss and some things you lose
by keeping your arm outstretched; and some things
you'll never know unless one, at least, knows you
like a close-up, in detail – blow by human blow.

As I Was Saying

Yes, madam, as a poet I *do* take myself seriously,
and, since I have a young, questioning family, I suppose
I should know something about English wild flowers:
the shape of their leaves, when this and that one grows,
how old mythologies attribute strange powers
to this or that one. Urban, I should mug up anew
the pleasant names: Butterbur, Ling, and Lady's Smock,
Jack-by-the Hedge, Cuckoo-Pint, and Feverfew,
even the Stinking Hellebore – all in that W. H. Smith book
I could bring home for myself (inscribed to my daughter)
to swot, to know which is this and which that one,
what honours the high cornfield, what the low water,
under the slow-pacing clouds and occasional sun of England.

But no! Done for in the ignorant suburb,
I'll drink Scotch, neurotically stare through glass
at the rainy lawn, at green stuff, nameless birds,
and let my daughter, madam, go to nature class.
I'll not compete with those nature poets you advance,
some in country dialect, and some in dialogue
with the country – few as calm as their words:
Wordsworth, Barnes, sad John Clare who ate grass.

Olfactory Pursuits

Often, unobserved, I smell my own hand.
I am searching for something forgotten.
I bang the door behind me, breathing in.

I think that a bitter or candied scent
is like a signpost pointing backwards
on which is writ no place and no distance.

So I walk towards a Verulamium,
your ruins or my ruins. The sun's ambushed:
fleeing on the ground the same, large shadow.

Look up. There's no smell to the colour blue.
The wind blew it right through the spaces
between clouds. Christ, what is it I'm after?

I dream, without sleeping, of things obscure,
of houses and streets and temples deserted
which, if once visited, I don't recall.

Here are a few stones instead of a wall,
and here broken stones instead of a house.
Hopelessly, with odours I conjoin.

My footfall echoes down old foundations,
buried mosaics, tomb tablets crumbled,
flints in the grass, your ruins or my ruins.

A man sniffs the back of his own hand,
moistens it with his mouth, to sniff again,
to think a blank; writes, 'The odour of stones.'

Halls

Halls of houses own a sweet biscuity smell;
and the carpet's frayed, the staircase lonely.

The landing light belongs to winter evenings.
When empty, all doors closed, the hall's itself.

It becomes an ear. Aware of a loud party
behind walls, and of cartilage clicking in a knee.

Between the porch and the head's eyes in a living room
it is the eight paces that can alter a man.

No wonder our grandfathers put clocks in halls,
and percussed barometers hopefully.

Lest the hall betray the host's formidable smile,
guests ushered in are not enticed to linger.

Later, guests leaving, slightly drunk, deranged,
neither know the hall nor the host, smileless.

What's detained by loitering, in gloomy halls,
near the leaded window and the telephone?

Well, nothing's defined by the keenest mind
aware of inviolate odours in halls.

Arcane, unparaphrasable halls.

On the Beach

HELEN: *I never went to Troy. Only a phantom went.*
MESSENGER: *What's this? All that suffering for nothing, simply for a cloud?*

Euripides, *Helena*

Yawning, I fold yesterday's newspaper
from England, and its news of Vietnam
which has had, and will have, a thousand names.
Then I lie back on the tourist sand.

Between the sun and the sea,
far from the sun and nearer to the sea,
a cloud, a single cloud, perhaps
a cloud by Zeus planted,
not much higher than those mountains.
A cloud or a woman's face?

A cloud. Helen never came to Troy.
Mad Paris kissed the pillow where she was not,
straddled the phantom he thought he saw,
and soiling the sheets, lay back still jerking,
'Helen, Helen,' satisfied.

I rise. I am level with the haunted sea,
now clear and unclear too deep for wine,
that breathes, because of the cloud, in shadow.
It wrinkles gradually towards me.
Surprise – in the débris of near waves breaking,
deluded voices sound within its sound.

As if two, clad like Trojan women,
curse Helen – not sick Paris and his cloud.
For Hector is dead and this one is his mother,
for Hector is dead and that one is his wife,
and his babe, alive, is being torn by beasts.

No camera clicks, no front-page photograph,
no great interview. I laugh aloud,
and hear nearby a transistor braying.
Altered by its dance tune, wrongly I translate:
'Helen, Helen, where are you?
Except for that cloud the sky is blue.'

Later, I walk back to the hotel thinking:
wherever women crouch beside their dead,
as Hecuba did, as Andromache,
motionless as sculpture till they raise their head,
with mouths wildly open to howl and curse,
now they call that cloud not Helen, no,
but a thousand names, and each one still untrue.

Again I gaze beyond the mountains' range.
In depths below the sun the cloud floats through,
soundless, around the world, it seems, forever.
I go into the hotel, and change.

Pathology of Colours

I know the colour rose, and it is lovely,
but not when it ripens in a tumour;
and healing greens, leaves and grass, so springlike,
in limbs that fester are not springlike.

I have seen red-blue tinged with hirsute mauve
in the plum-skin face of a suicide.
I have seen white, china white almost, stare
from behind the smashed windscreen of a car.

And the criminal, multi-coloured flash
of an H-bomb is no more beautiful
than an autopsy when the belly's opened –
to show cathedral windows never opened.

So in the simple blessing of a rainbow,
in the bevelled edge of a sunlit mirror,
I have seen, visible, Death's artefact
like a soldier's ribbon on a tunic tacked.

The Sheds

Articulate suffering may be a self-admiring,
but what of the long sheds where a man could only howl?
How quickly, then, silhouettes came running
across the evening fields, knee deep in mist.

Or what of nights when the sheds disappeared,
fields empty, a night landscape unrhetorical
until the moon, as pale as pain, holed a cloud?
As if men slept, dreamed, as others touched on lights.

Hunt the Thimble

Hush now. You cannot describe it.

Is it like heavy rain falling,
and lights going on, across the fields,
in the new housing estate?

Cold, cold. Too domestic, too
temperate, too devoid of history.

Is it like a dark windowed street at night,
the houses uncurtained, the street deserted?

Colder. You are getting colder,
and too romantic, too dream-like.
You cannot describe it.

The brooding darkness then
that breeds inside a cathedral
of a provincial town in Spain.

In Spain, also, but not Spanish.
In England, if you like, but not English.
It remains, even when obscure, perpetually.
Aged, but ageless, you cannot describe it.
No, you are cold, altogether too cold.

Aha – the blue sky over Ampourias,
the blue sky over Lancashire for that matter . . .

You cannot describe it.

. . . obscured by clouds?
I must know what you mean.

Hush, hush.

Like those old men in hospital dying,
who, unaware strangers stand around their bed,
stare obscurely, for a long moment,
at one of their own hands raised –
which perhaps is bigger than the moon again –
and then, drowsy, wandering, shout out, 'Mama'.

Is it like that? Or hours after that even:
the darkness inside a dead man's mouth?

No, no, I have told you:
you are cold, and you cannot describe it.

A Night Out

Friends recommended the new Polish film
at the Academy in Oxford Street.
So we joined the ever melancholy queue
of cinemas. A wind blew faint suggestions
of rain towards us, and an accordion.
Later, uneasy, in the velvet dark
we peered through the cut-out oblong window
at the spotlit drama of our nightmares:
images of Auschwitz almost authentic,
the human obscenity in close-up.
Certainly we could imagine the stench.

Resenting it, we forgot the barbed wire
was but a prop and could not scratch an eye;
those striped victims merely actors like us.
We saw the Camp orchestra assembled,
we heard the solemn gaiety of Bach,
scored by the loud arrival of an engine,
its impotent cry and its guttural trucks.
We watched, as we munched milk chocolate,
trustful children, no older than our own,
strolling into the chambers without fuss,
while smoke, black and curly, oozed from chimneys.

Afterwards, at a loss, we sipped coffee
in a bored espresso bar nearby
saying very little. You took off one glove.
Then to the comfortable suburb swiftly
where, arriving home, we garaged the car.
We asked the au pair girl from Germany
if anyone had phoned at all, or called,
and, of course, if the children had woken.
Reassured, together we climbed the stairs,
undressed together, and naked together,
in the dark, in the marital bed, made love.

Fah

Not to irritate him did you sit,
frequenting one note, at the piano stool,
over and over; resting your finger
on that one sound till that sound vanished.
Yes, you played it again after it faded,
then felt it again and played it again
as he became anxious, a tightening nerve.

For that one sound, at first amiable,
soon touched down on the whole feminine,
far world of hermetic lamentations.
You sat there, it seemed, absent, unaware,
like a child (certainly without menace)
and fathomed it again and played it again,
a small desperation this side of death.

Not to confront him with choices
did you play: he did not quit the room quietly;
he did not shout out abruptly, 'Stop it';
he would not say with compassion, 'My dear . . .';
but only coughed behind his hand politely.
Odd, then, that he coughed again and again,
and could not stop although the tears came.

Even

Coffee-time morning, down the gradient,
like a shop window for Jehovah,
they pass my gate to the synagogue
as Saturday skies vault over.

Dressed like that they lose their charm
who carry prayer books, wear a hat.
I don't like them, I don't like them,
and guilty fret – just thinking that.

I don't like them, I don't like them –
again the dodgy thought comes through:
could it be I am another
tormented, anti-semite Jew?

No. Next morning on the Sunday,
processions uphill, piebald, lurch,
in the opposite direction,
towards the ivy-covered church.

Look, dressed for Christ and hygiene,
they glare back like Swiss-Germans
spruced and starched in piety,
and fag on slow as sermons.

All God's robots lose their charm
who carry prayer books, wear a hat.
I don't like them, I don't like them,
and feel less guilty thinking that.

So let both ministers propound
the pathology of religions,
and pass my gate you zealots of
scrubbed, excremental visions.

The Ballad of Oedipus Sex

I pull the knife out of my chest,
    the light begins to fail.
  Don't read the Sunday papers:
    myself will tell the tale.
Forget the printed photograph
    that makes me look a freak.
  Oedipus wrote the headlines
    for longer than a week,

      singing hey diddle diddlio,
        hey diddle diddle dee.

It was midnight on the river,
    the sky a domino.
  I pushed my gloomy father
    into gloomy coils below.
Such a silence on the river,
    you could hear the oars creak.
  Oedipus wrote the headlines
    for longer than a week,

      singing hey diddle diddlio,
        hey diddle diddle dee.

I rowed straight home to stepmother
    and seized her in my bed.
  A moth was in the lampshade,
    the light was in my head:
some like girls contemporary
    but I like them antique.
  Oedipus wrote the headlines
    for longer than a week,

    singing hey diddle diddlio,
      hey diddle diddle dee.

When, dripping, the ghost of father,
    a hatchet in his hand,
  appeared on the threshold
    I found I couldn't stand;
though true love may last forever
    for me it turned out bleak.
  Oedipus wrote the headlines
    for longer than a week,

    singing hey diddle diddlio,
      hey diddle diddle dee.

I telephoned the analyst
    and conned him for a date.
  He listened to my dreaming,
    a father surrogate.
I arose and cut his throat then
    from bloody cheek to cheek.
  Oedipus wrote the headlines
    for longer than a week,

        singing hey diddle diddlio,
            hey diddle diddle dee.

The analyst had a lady,
    she never said a word;
  for when I gazed into her eyes
    a transference occurred.
So I took her to the river
    and now she's up the creek.
  Oedipus wrote the headlines
    for longer than a week,

        singing hey diddle diddlio,
            hey diddle diddle dee.

Six policemen came a-knocking,
    the door they tried to force.
  I'd have horsewhipped the lot if
    I'd only had a horse.
Six bullets through the keyhole,
    six policemen sprung a leak.
  Oedipus wrote the headlines
    for longer than a week,

      singing hey diddle diddlio,
        hey diddle diddle dee.

I was sheltered by Jocasta,
    a widow with catarrh.
  'Your sins be white as snow,' she thrilled,
    'Long as you love your ma.
Forget my past, my pet, my poodle,
    and let me be your peke.'
  Oedipus wrote the headlines
    for longer than a week,

      singing hey diddle diddlio,
        hey diddle diddle dee.

So of Jocasta now I sing
    like any swooning bard:
  the very wrinkles of her face,
    her arteries so hard.
Mock if you must! You don't know her!
    Or her veteran's technique.
  Oedipus wrote the headlines
    for longer than a week,

    singing hey diddle diddlio,
      hey diddle diddle dee.

A son we had and loved him,
    I loved him more than best;
  but on his thirteenth birthday
    he knifed me in the chest.
At the Golden Cock in Fleet Street
    they tell how Greek met Greek.
  Oedipus wrote the headlines
    for longer than a week,

    singing hey diddle diddlio,
      hey diddle diddle dee.

Since Sophocles and Shakespeare
      divined our human laws,
   I've gone bleeding down the aisles
      to inTERminable applause.
Now I'm dying, Jocasta, dying,
      my plot was not unique:
Oedipus wrote the headlines
      for longer than a week,

      singing hey diddle diddlio,
         hey diddle diddle . . . Dada?

A Suburban Episode

Since you telephoned to say – in a tiny voice –
(how servile you are) intruders intruders walk
in pairs across the back lawn (I'm sorry, you say)
I say heartily, too heartily perhaps,
do not lock yourself in oh dear no,
go out, shout, challenge them, ask them why.

Since you say that some — the most impertinent —
and therefore you think (wrongly) the most important,
for instance, those in plum-coloured blazers,
are cutting down your tulips, snip snip snip,
one by one with small scissors, small nail-scissors,
I say with formidable aggression
stride out, ask them for credentials, stop them;
but remember walk with very long steps.

Still that is not your nature (you *are* pitiful)
and rightly you remind me you are a stranger
in this city. As for me, well you know my name,
all ratepayers know my name. I am important,
I am Vice-Chairman of the Watch Committee,
so wait for me, I say, we'll tackle them together.

So later, together, I who have been decorated
by the Queen, and you poor, timid foreigner,
swing back the door. (Whistling a merry tune
it was I, naturally, who turned the rusty key.)
But, alas, there are no intruders on your lawn
nor tulips growing either, scathed or unscathed.

A tree, crashing, catapults a bird as we stand
conspiratorially together in the dusk,
you fiddling with your spectacles, and I
just one inch above the lawn, exactly one inch, I say.
And there were intruders here you say,
and there were tulips there you say.

Do not apologize. For believe me
I believe you. I know your nation (I mean your nature)
and how cunning things can be, damnably cunning.
Why, have I not heard, even I, first cousin
of the mayor, heard in the night a stone falling?
No ordinary stone either, scraping the sheer ledges,
and later many stones, boulders even, leaping down
out of earshot, down the sides of hell.

Not Adlestrop

Not Adlestrop, no – besides, the name
hardly matters. Nor did I languish in June heat.
Simply, I stood, too early, on the empty platform,
and the wrong train came in slowly, surprised, stopped.
Directly facing me, from a window,
a very, *very* pretty girl leaned out.

        When I, all instinct,
stared at her, she, all instinct, inclined her head away
as if she'd divined the much married life in me,
or as if she might spot, up platform,
some unlikely familiar.

For my part, under the clock, I continued
my scrutiny with unmitigated pleasure.
And she knew it, she certainly knew it, and would not
glance at me in the silence of not Adlestrop.

Only when the train heaved noisily, only
when it jolted, when it slid away, only *then*,
daring and secure, she smiled back at my smile,
and I, daring and secure, waved back at her waving.
And so it was, all the way down the hurrying platform
as the train gathered atrocious speed
towards Oxfordshire or Gloucestershire.

In Llandough Hospital

'To hasten night would be humane,'
I, a doctor, beg a doctor,
for still the darkness will not come —
his sunset slow, his first star pain.

I plead: 'We know another law.
For one maimed bird we'd do as much,
and if a creature need not suffer
must he, for etiquette, endure?'

Earlier, 'Go now, son,' my father said,
for my sake commanding me.
Now, since death makes victims of us all,
he's thin as Auschwitz in that bed.

Still his courage startles me. The fears
I'd have, he has none. Who'd save
Socrates from the hemlock,
or Winkelried from the spears?

We quote or misquote in defeat,
in life, and at the camps of death.
Here comes the night with all its stars,
bright butchers' hooks for man and meat.

I grasp his hand so fine, so mild,
which still is warm surprisingly,
not a handshake either, father,
but as I used to when a child.

And as a child can't comprehend
what germinates philosophy,
so like a child I question why
night with stars, then night without end.

Two Small Stones

After the therapy of the grave ritual
(mourners who weep circumspectly weep less long)
'A fine man.' No-one snarled the priest was wrong.
Relatives pressed limp hands, filed out, heads bowed,
emotional as opera singers. But mute their song.

I do not know why I picked up two small stones
(bits of broken sky trailed on the gravel path)
and dropped them in my pocket. No epitaph,
no valediction pardoned me. Why didn't I cry,
and why won't I throw these stones away? Don't laugh.

Not Beautiful

In all hiroshimas, in raw and raving voices,
   live skeletons of the Camp, flies hugging faeces,
      in war, in famine, he'd find the beautiful.

Being saintly, his vocation was to find it
   at the dying bedside, in the disrobing dead.
      And what he did, they said, you should be trying.

Well, once, while dissecting a nerve in a cadaver
   my cigarette dropped, fell into its abdomen.
      I picked it up. I puffed out the smoke of hell.

Yet still was not fit for time to come: the freehold grave,
   things run over like slush all bloody and throbbing –
      for though they were dumb, not beautiful, I said.

It's the parable again of the three wise men:
   the first who, with finger and thumb, tweaked his nostrils,
      and the second who pressed his eyes to his palms,

whilst the third, the wisest, cried, 'Oh what beautiful,
    white teeth have these vermin which died.' Homo sum,
        etc., but the third was divine (as they said).

One sees the good point, of course, and may admire it;
    but, sometimes, I think that to curse is more sacred
        than to pretend by affirming. And offend.

Interview with a Spirit Healer

Smiling, he says no man should fear the tomb
for where we fade the grass is greener.
Listen! Someone coughs in his waiting room;
then, from upstairs, the suburban howl of
the made ghost in a vacuum cleaner.

With nude emotion, he names the miracles
as hip fans would football matches.
His voice catches on the incurably cured
whose letters, testimonials, conclude,
'. . . though the doctors gave me up as hopeless'.

His tragic venue, those frayed English spas:
Cheltenham, Leamington, Tunbridge, Bath,
where depressed male Tories, on their sticks,
guzzle in chromium and maroon hotel bars
which seem more empty when people whisper.

He murmurs, 'Love,' which could be disturbing,
also 'Spirit guides.' Look, his upraised hand
shows me neither its knuckles nor its palm,
and, like a candle in daytime burning,
seems but a sign ethereal as a psalm.

Goodbye! His spirituality is too inbred,
too indelible like a watermark;
and I, gross sceptic, hired by a paper,
prefer my dead to be in the dark.
Goodbye. His eyes, Mary's blue, stare at vapour.

Let him, in faith, stare on. I loathe his trade,
the disease and the sanctimonious lie
that cannot cure the disease. My need,
being healthy, is not faith; but to curse the day
I became mortal the night my father died.

Give Me Your Hands

Scared trees, hissing in the garden,
can't hear human voices harden.
I can: my two neighbours quarrel.

Mine! Mine! Nothing to do with me.
Once more I flex my head to see
the latest Sunday photograph.

In Vietnam, beneath scarred trees,
unreal the staring casualties.
Of course I care. What good is that?

Faint in the hall the telephone goes.
As I approach, how loud it grows.
I lift up a voice saying, 'Doctor?'

So in a room I do not know
I hold a hand I do not know
for hours. Again a dry old hand.

There's something else that I must do,
for some other thing is crying too
in chaos, near, without a name.

Anonymities

I

Christ, a spaceman, diving *up*,
head first to heaven – crazy, absurd,
even though painted by Titian.

Outside the Palace of the Dukes
the dying beggar of Urbino
accosted us.

His blue, aryan eye surprised us.
He was offensive, having no name.

2

At Gradara, perhaps,
even Paolo and Francesca
would walk in their electric ghosts,
pace the battlements, twice nightly,
though I saw no advertisement.

A mile down the road from the castle,
before the level crossing, look!
. . . the war cemetery.
No ghost would stir there being nameless.
I held my dark glasses in my hand;
the air, therefore, no longer khaki.

What a real green prettiness
devised poppies not made of paper.
Silence seemed obligatory.
Afterwards, I pulled the starter three times:
the usual choking noise of an imbecile
before the car edged forward.

My sun-glasses now back in front of my eyes,
I thought: 'Soldier . . . soldiers . . .
don't you know yet? Your uniform even . . .
Khaki is the colour of shit . . .'

3

At 4 o'clock on the autostrada,
hot, very hot, and far to the left the mountains,
somewhere between Bologna and Milan,
cars unreeled in a fragmented,
rising and fading hysteria.

It happened then:

a squealing, a destroying noise
through the khaki afternoon.
Coming towards us from the other side
a car was heaving into pieces,
through air undulating like cheap glass,
lancinating metal flying
across the road, lasciviously.

But, 'Press on,' I thought, and swerved
in the buckled sunlight to avoid another car
which in decent mercy had braked in front.
'Cool,' I thought, 'I am cool in a crisis,'
feeling proud, omnipotent, self-absorbed.

Later, of course, grew ashamed when 'Kaput'
said the ambulance man, having no English.
Now we peered through real glass that was flawed.
One eye, blue as Urbino, could not blink;
as for the other, not an eye at all
but the material of a poppy.
And flies sat on the meat.

4

In Milan, next morning, I, a tourist,
visited 'the wedding cake' cathedral,
and felt nothing.
All that vain, perpendicular magnificence,
that yearning melodrama of glass and stone,
how it towered, how it strained,
but, of course, could not fly to heaven.
I felt nothing.

For 200 lire, on the vertigo of its roofs,
other tourists also clambered.
Amongst the monstrous gargoyles I laughed, raggedly,
and said, with the genius of an idiot,
'What a wedding cake when the bride is Death!'

Down, down, angled down below,
on the square, the smallest people ever
scurried ridiculously.
God-like, I blinked from a large, ceremonial eye.
With a long leg, my shoe could have stamped one out.
It wouldn't have mattered.
Not knowing whom.

The Motto

Who heard the no thing to write nothing down?
Who switched the record player on instead?

Whose slate-blue smoke idled to the lampshade?
Who killed his cigarette and went to bed?

Who, half the night, could not sleep for Mozart
And thought to hell with all those classic gems?

Who said without such music in the head
A man's more fit for stratagems?

He bungled though – when music sought him out.
He whistled still, but did not know what for.

His stick in winter doodled in the snow;
Be visited, expect nothing, and endure.

The Smile Was

one thing I waited for always
after the shouting
after the palaver
the perineum stretched to pain
the parched voice of the midwife
        Push! Push!

and I can't and the rank
sweet smell of the gas
and
              I can't
as she whiffed cotton wool
inside her head
as the hollow stones of gas
dragged
         her
              down
from the lights above
to the river-bed, to the real stones.
              Push! Push!
as she floated up again
muscles tensed, to the electric
till the little head was crowned;
and I shall wait again
for the affirmation.

For it is such:
that effulgent, tender, satisfied
smile of a woman
who, for the first time,
hears the child crying the world
for the very first time.

That agreeable, radiant smile –
no man can smile it
no man can paint it
as it develops without fail,
after the gross, physical, knotted,
granular, bloody endeavour.
    Such a pure spirituality, from all that!
It occupies the face
and commands it.
            Out of relief
you say, reasonably thinking of the reasonable,
swinging lightness of any reprieve,
the joy of it, almost helium in the head.

            So wouldn't you?
And truly there's always the torture of the unknown.
There's always the dream of pregnant women,
blood of the monster in the blood of the child;
and we all know of generations lost
like words faded on a stone,
of minds blank or wild with genetic mud.
            And couldn't you
smile like that?

Not like that, no, never,
not with such indefinable
dulcitude as that.
And so she smiles
with eyes as brown as a dog's
or eyes blue-mad as a doll's
it makes no odds
whore, beauty, or bitch,
it makes no odds
illimitable chaste happiness
in that smile
as new life-in-the-world
for the first time cries the world.
No man can smile like that.

2

No man can paint it.
Da Vinci sought it out
yet was far, far, hopelessly.
Leonardo, you only made
Mona Lisa look six months gone!

I remember the smile of the Indian.
I told him
        Fine, finished,
you are cured
and he sat there smiling sadly.
Any painter could paint it
the smile of a man resigned
saying
        Thank you, doctor,
you have been kind
and then, as in melodrama,
        How long
have I to live?
The Indian smiling, resigned,
all the fatalism of the East.

So one starts again, also smiling,
        All is well
you are well, you are cured.
And the Indian still smiling
his assignations with death
still shaking his head, resigned.
        Thank you
for telling me the truth, doctor.
Two months? Three months?

And beginning again
   and again
whatever I said, thumping the table,
however much I reassured him
the more he smiled the conspiratorial
smile of a damned, doomed man.

Now a woman, a lady, a whore,
a bitch, a beauty, whatever,
   the child's face crumpled
as she becomes the mother,
she smiles differently, ineffably.

3

As different as
the smile of my colleague,
his eyes reveal it,
his ambiguous assignations,
good man, good surgeon,
whose smile arrives of its own accord
   from nowhere
like flies to a dead thing
when he makes the first incision.

Who draws a line of blood
across the soft, white flesh
as if something beneath,
desiring violence, had beckoned him;
who draws a ritual wound,
a calculated wound
to heal – to heal,
but still a wound –
good man, good surgeon,
his smile as luxuriant
as the smile of Peter Lorre.

So is the smile of my colleague,
the smile of a man
secretive behind the mask.

The smile of war.

But the smile, the smile
of the new mother,
what
     an extraordinary
          open thing
               it is.

4

Walking home tonight I saw
an ordinary occurrence
hardly worth remarking on:
an unhinged star, a streaking gas,
and I thought how lovely
destruction is when it is far.
Ruined it slid
on the dead dark towards fiction:
its lit world disappeared
phut, through one punched hole or another,
slipped unseen down the back of the sky
into another time.

Never,
not for one single death
can I forget we die with the dead,
and the world dies with us;
yet
in one, lonely,
small child's birth
all the tall dead rise
to break the crust of the imperative earth.

No wonder the mother smiles
a wonder like that,
a lady, a whore, a bitch, a beauty.
Eve smiled like that
when she heard Seth cry out Abel's dark,
earth dark, the first dark
eeling on the deep sea-bed,
struggling on the real stones.
Hecuba, Cleopatra, Lucretia Borgia,
Annette Vallon smiled like that.

They all, still, smile like that,
when the child first whimpers like a seagull
the ancient smile reasserts itself
instinct with a return
so outrageous and so shameless;
the smile the smile
always the same
               an uncaging
                   a freedom.

Mysteries

At night, I do not know who I am
when I dream, when I am sleeping.

Awakened, I hold my breath and listen:
a thumbnail scratches the other side of the wall.

At midday, I enter a sunlit room
to observe the lamplight on for no reason.

I should know by now that few octaves can be heard,
that a vision dies from being too long stared at;

that the whole of recorded history even
is but a little gossip in a great silence;

that a magnesium flash cannot illumine,
for one single moment, the invisible.

I do not complain. I start with the visible
and am startled by the visible.

Forgotten

That old country I once said I'd visit
when older. Can no one tell me its name?
Odd to have forgotten what it is called.
I would recognize the name if I heard it.
So many times I have searched the atlas
with a prowling convex lens – to no avail.

I know the geography of the great world
has changed; the war, the peace, the deletions
of places – red pieces gone forever,
and names of countries altered forever:
Gold Coast Ghana, Persia become Iran,
Siam Thailand, and Hell now Vietnam.

People deleted. Must I sleep again to reach it,
to find the back door opening to a field,
a barking of dogs, and a path that leads back?
One night in pain, the dead middle of night,
will I awake again, know who I am,
the man from somewhere else, and the place's name?

An Old Commitment

Long ago my kinsmen slain in battle,
swart flies on all their pale masks feeding.

I had a cause then. Surely I had a cause?
I was for them and they were for me.

Now, when I recall why, what, who,
I think the thought that is as blank as stone.

Travelling this evening, I focus on the back
of brightness, on that red spot wavering.

Behind it, what have I forgotten? It goes
where the red spot goes, rising, descending.

I only describe a sunset, a car travelling
on a swerving mountain road, that's all.

Arriving too late, I approach the unlit dark.
Those who loiter outside exits and entrances

so sadly, so patiently, even they have departed.
And I am no ghost and this place is in ruins.

'Black,' I call softly to one dead but beloved,
'black, black,' wanting the night to reply . . .

                                    . . . 'Black.'

Demo against the Vietnam War, 1968

Praise just one thing in London, he challenged,
as if everybody, everything, owned a minus,
was damnable, and the Inner Circle led to hell;
and I thought, allowed one slot only,
what, in October, would I choose?

Not the blurred grasslands of a royal, moody park
where great classy trees lurk in mist;
not the secretive Thames either, silvering
its slow knots through the East End –
sooty scenes, good for Antonioni panning soft
atmospheric shots, emblems of isolation,
prologue to the elegiac Square, the house where,
suddenly, lemon oblongs spring to windows.

Nor would I choose the stylized catalogue
of torment in the National Gallery.
Better that tatty group under Nelson's column,
their home-made banners held aloft,
their small cries of 'Peace, Peace,' impotent;
also the moment with the tannoy turned off,
the thudding wings of pigeons audible,
the shredding fountains, once again, audible.

So praise to the end of the march,
their songs, their jargon, outside the Embassy.
Yes, this I'd choose: their ardour, their naïveté,
violence of commitment, cruelty of devotion,
'We shall not be moved, We shall overcome' –
despite sullen police concealed in vans
waiting for arclights to fail, for furtive darkness,
and camera-teams, dismantled, all breezing home.

Haloes

Of course haloes are out of fashion.
The commissar is in the castle,
the haemophylic king plays golf
in exile. Feudal days, no more.
Once martyrs were a glut on the market,
now famine faces sink in Asia;
now lamps switched on in drawing rooms
reveal suffering saints no longer there –
as if they had leapt down from walls
leaving behind them halo-tissue.

Such a round shining on walls!
Such a bleeding of intense light!
And all those haloes in hymns of paint,
in museums, in galleries, counterfeit.
Still we appease the old deities –
else we would be like madmen laughing
in public buildings, apparent joy
where rational people speak in whispers;
else saints would never look so ecstatic
in chiaroscuro, on starvation diet.

The Pope does not eat his own entrails
with a golden fork, nor his secretary
cease from phoning the Stock Exchange.
Haloes set men alight in Prague.
Here crowds prefer to shout, 'Easy, Easy,'
at a poisoned green pitch in floodlight.
Pop star, film star, space man, gangster,
move smilingly from camera to camera
seldom to become ritual torches.
Each worth a million, say the guides.

Rightly we are suspicious of haloes
and heroes, of thorns and royal tiaras.
Day and night, an H-bomb circles the world
and Fatty and his henchmen walk
on marble floors, their heritage.
No wonder important men lift up
their hats politely, revealing bald heads.
No-one minds. Their skins have healed.
Think of wall lamps switched off
savagely, all haloes fleeing.

Moon Object

After the astronaut's intrusion of moonlight, after
the metal flag, the computer-speeches – this little booty.

Is it really from the moon? Identify it if you can.
Test it, blue-eyed scientist, between finger and thumb.

Through a rainy city a car continues numb.
Its radio blanks out beneath a bridge.

In a restaurant, your colleague with a cold
is trying to taste his own saliva.

On the school piano, your wife's index finger
sinks the highest note. She hears the sound of felt.

Blue eyes, let your own finger and your thumb
slip and slide about it devilishly.

Don't you feel the gravity of the moon?
Say a prayer for the dead and murmur a vow.

Change your white coat for a purple cloak
and cage yourself a peacock or a gnat.

No, rational, you sniff it. But some holes in your front-brain
have been scooped out. A moon-howling dog would know.

Blue eyes, observe it again. See its dull appearance
and be careful: it could be cursed, it could be sleeping.

Awake, it might change colour like a lampshade
turned on, seething – suddenly moon-plugged.

Scientist, something rum has happened to you.
Your right and left eyes have been switched around.

Back home, if you dialled your own number now,
a shameless voice would reply, 'Who? Who?'

Peachstone

I do not visit his grave. He is not there.
Out of hearing, out of reach. I miss him here,
seeing hair grease at the back of a chair
near a firegrate where his spit sizzled,
or noting, in the cut-glass bowl, a peach.

For that night his wife brought him a peach,
his favourite fruit, while the sick light glowed,
and his slack, dry mouth sucked, sucked, sucked,
with dying eyes closed – perhaps for her sake –
till bright as blood the peachstone showed.

Three Street Musicians

Three street musicians in mourning overcoats
worn too long, shake money boxes this morning,
then, afterwards, play their suicide notes.

The violinist in chic, black spectacles, blind,
the stout tenor with a fake Napoleon stance,
and the loony flautist following behind,

they try to importune us, the busy living,
who hear melodic snatches of music hall
above unceasing waterfalls of traffic.

Yet if anything can summon back the dead
it is the old-time sound, old obstinate tunes,
such as they achingly render and suspend:

'The Minstrel Boy', 'Roses of Picardy'.
No wonder cemeteries are full of silences
and stones keep down the dead that they defend.

Stones too light! Airs irresistible!
Even a dog listens, one paw raised, while the stout,
loud man amazes with nostalgic notes – though half boozed

and half clapped out. And, as breadcrumbs thrown
on the ground charm sparrows down from nowhere,
now, suddenly, there are too many ghosts about.

Portrait of the Artist as a Middle-Aged Man

(3.30 a.m., January 1st)

Pure Xmas card below – street under snow,
under lamplight. My children curl asleep,
my wife also moans from depths too deep
with all her shutters closed and half her life.
And I? I, sober now, come down the stairs
to eat an apple, to taste the snow in it,
to switch the light on at the maudlin time.

Habitual living room, where the apple-flesh
turns brown after the bite, oh half my life
has gone to pot. And, now, too tired for sleep,
I count up the Xmas cards childishly,
assessing, *Jesus*, how many friends I've got!

A New Diary

This clerk-work, this first January chore
of who's in, who's out. A list to think about
when absences seem to shout, Scandal! Outrage!
So turning to the blank, prefatory page
I transfer most of the names and phone tags
from last year's diary. True, Meadway, Speedwell,
Mountview, are computer-changed into numbers,
and already their pretty names begin to fade
like Morwenna, Julie, Don't-Forget-Me-Kate,
grassy summer girls I once swore love to.
These, whispering others and time will date.

Cancelled, too, a couple someone else betrayed,
one man dying, another mind in rags.
And remembering them my clerk-work flags,
bitterly flags, for all lose, no-one wins,
those in, those out, *this* at the heart of things?
So I stop, ask: whom should I commemorate,
and who, perhaps, is crossing out my name now
from some future diary? Oh my God,
Morwenna, Julie, don't forget me, Kate.

Miss Book World

We, the judges, a literary lot,
peep-tom legitimately at these beauties,
give marks for legs and breasts, make remarks
low or pompous like most celebrities;
not that we are, but they imagine us so
who parade blatantly as camera-lights flash
crazily for a glossy page and cash.

Perhaps some girls entered for a giggle,
but all walk slave-like in this ritual fuss
of unfunny compère, funny applause,
spotlit dream-girls displayed, a harem for us;
not that they are, but we imagine them so,
with Miss Book World herself just barely flawed,
almost perfect woman, almost perfect fraud.

The illusion over, half the contestants
still fancy themselves in their knock-out pose,
while we literati return to the real
world of fancy, great poetry and prose;
not that it is, but we imagine it so,
great vacant visions in which we delight,
as if we see the stars not only at night.

The Death of Aunt Alice

Aunt Alice's funeral was orderly,
each mourner correct, dressed in decent black,
not one balding relative berserk with an axe.
Poor Alice, where's your opera-ending?
For alive you relished high catastrophe,
your bible Page One of a newspaper.

You talked of typhoid when we sat to eat;
Fords on the M4, mangled, upside down,
just when we were going for a spin;
and, at London airport, as you waved us off,
how you fatigued us with 'metal fatigue',
vague shapes of Boeings bubbling under seas.

Such disguises and such transformations!
Even trees were but factories for coffins,
rose bushes decoys to rip boys' eyes with thorns.
Sparrows became vampires, spiders had designs,
and your friends also grew SPECTACULAR,
none to bore you by dying naturally.

A. had both kidneys removed in error
at Guy's. 'And such a clever surgeon too.'
B., one night, fell screaming down a liftshaft.
'Poor fellow, he never had a head for heights.'
C., so witty, so feminine, 'Pity
she ended up in a concrete mixer.'

But now, never again, Alice, will you utter
gory admonitions as some do oaths.
Disasters that lit your eyes will no more
unless, trembling up there, pale saints listen
to details of their bloody martyrdoms,
all their tall stories, your eternity.

Car Journeys

1   *Down the M4*

Me! dutiful son going back to South Wales, this time afraid
to hear my mother's news. Too often, now, her friends are
    disrobed,
and my aunts and uncles, too, go into the hole, one by one.
The beautiful face of my mother is in its ninth decade.

Each visit she tells me the monotonous story of clocks.
'Oh dear,' I say, or 'how funny,' till I feel my hair turning grey
for I've heard that perishable one two hundred times
    before –
like the rugby 'amateurs' with golden sovereigns in their
    socks.

Then the Tawe ran fluent and trout-coloured over stones
    stonier,
more genuine; then Annabella, my mother's mother, spoke
    Welsh
with such an accent the village said, 'Tell the truth, fach,
you're no Jewess. *They're* from the Bible. *You're* from
    Patagonia!'

I'm driving down the M4 again under bridges that leap
over me then shrink in my side mirror. Ystalyfera is farther
than smoke and God further than all distance known. I
    whistle
no hymn but an old Yiddish tune my mother knows.
It won't keep.

2   *Incident on a summer night*

The route not even in the AA book.
I'm nowhere, I thought, driving slowly
because of the raw surface of the lane
that developed between converging hedges;
then, soon, fabulous in the ghastly wash
of headlights, a naked man approached
crying without inhibition, one hand to his face,
his somehow familiar mouth agape.

Surely he could see me?
From the two moth-filled headlights
surely he would draw back, change his pace?
This road to Paradise, I muttered.
At last I passed him or say, rather, he passed me.
Afterwards, the accelerating lane widened
and long lights fumbled, momentarily,
hedges, hurtling gate, country wall, amazing tree.

3   *I sit in my parked car*

And they, too, seem like images from sleep:
this Asian child and shadow
playing on a rubbish heap;
that old man incognito
preaching to the pigeons.
'Kill the Reds,' he says, 'kill the Reds.'
I wind up the car window.

Nearby, sunlight on a broken bottle
throws trinket colours on a stone,
but the ancient man in smoked glasses
walks to the right alone
mouthing a forgotten language,
walks out of sight, off the page.

And I? I leave the car, feel dizzy —
even the plastic seating's hot.
Grounded pigeons purr their gutturals,
the pistons in their heads are busy.
When the door slams its small shot
the pigeons reach for the sky,
the shadow chases the child.

In Hotel Insomnia, once, at dawn,
I thought I heard those pigeons' wings
whirring outside my numbered door.
It was only the lift gone wild.
Up and down on a nightmare ride
its gates opened at each floor,
gates of ivory or of horn:
no Asian child, nor ancient man.
Nobody at all inside.

4   *Driving home*

Opposing carbeams wash my face.
Such flickerings hypnotize. To keep awake
I listen to the BBC through cracklings
of static, fade-outs under bridges,
to a cool expert who, in lower case,
computes and graphs 'the ecological
disasters that confront the human race.'

Almost immediately (ironically?),
I see blue flashing lights ahead and brake
before a car accordioned, floodlit, men heaving
at a stretcher, an ambulance oddly angled, tame, in wait.
Afterwards, silent, I drive home cautiously
where, late, the eyes of my youngest child
flicker dreamily, and are full of television.

'He's waited up,' his mother says, 'to say goodnight.'
My son smiles briefly. Such emotion! I surprise
myself and him when I hug him tight.

A Note Left on the Mantelpiece

(For his wife)

Attracted by their winning names I chose
Little Yid and *Welsh Bard*; years later backed
the swanky jockeys, and still thought I lacked
inspiration, the uncommon touch, not
mere expertise. Each way, I paid in prose.

Always the colours and stadiums beckoned
till, on the nose, at Goodwood, the high gods
jinxed the favourite despite the odds.
Addict that I was, live fool and dead cert.
His velvet nostrils lagged a useless second.

A poet should have studied style not form
(sweet, I regret the scarcity of roses)
but by Moses and by the nine Muses
I'll no more. Each cruising nag is a beast
so other shirts can keep the centaur warm.

Adieu, you fading furlongs of boozing,
hoarse voices at Brighton, white rails, green course.
Conclusion? Why, not only the damned horse
but whom it's running against matters.
By the way, apologies for losing.

A Faithful Wife

*(A letter written by an Egyptian lady during the reign of
Amenhotep III, about 1385 BCE)*

To my husband, my lord,
whose caravans lodge in Canaan,
whose sperm has not stiffened,
for three long months, my bed-linen,
say:
at the feet of my husband,
as before the king, the sun–god,
seven times and seven times
I fall.
For I am an obedient
of my husband, my lord.

When I keep my head still
moving my two eyes this way
it is dark;
when I keep my head still
moving my two eyes that way
it is dark;
but when I gaze in front,
towards my lord, it is dazzle,
it is the spirit on the wall
flat as a sunbeam:
it is the time of the short shadows.

Further: all seems tasteless
like the white of an egg
since my lord departed.
Thus ask my falcon, my husband,
to send for his servant, as promised,
to journey on the stony heat
across the camel-coloured desert
even to the shrewd wells.
For I have placed the yoke
of my husband, my lord,
upon my neck and I bear it.

In the whirling dust-storm,
a brick may move
from beneath its companions.
When the night grows with jackals
a dog may move
from his sick master.
But send for me and I shall not move
from beneath the shadow
of my husband, my lord,
as that shadow will not move
from his two feet.

Yet my lord sends no report,
neither good nor evil.
Has he gone to the land of Hatti,
or to the region of the bedouins?
Does he take care of his chariot?
When the first three stars appear
does he sleep each evening
with a piece of wool upon him?
Or has the foe raided his caravans,
the night guards drunk, my lord inert?
Very anxious is thy servant.

Oh may this tablet find him safe
in Joppa, in the meadows
blossoming in their season:
else let the dust follow his chariot
like smoke, and let the god, Amon, keep
all those tracks that zag between
the rising and the setting sun
free from ambuscade,
free for my lord whose speeches are
gathered together on my tongue,
and remain upon my lips.

The Bereaved

I

Once his voice had been so thrilling,
the twelve women all agreed. Off and on TV
he was charming, he was charismatic,
yet without side. He was their pin-up.

But now his incomprehensible language
when he spoke (which was rare);
the way he would stare into chasms of space
as if Eurydice were there; or would suddenly

howl out an emptiness – that was too much
(a man should not dream of maggots too long)
that was ridiculous, even frightening, they said,
the twelve women, reasonably moving towards him.

2

Twelve women pulling him,
twelve women screaming,
kicking, scratching, pulling at him,
until on the ground, at last,
he was being smothered,
bitten by women's teeth,
his eyes pushed in by women's thumbs.

Afterwards, the cyanosed figure
on the ground, what was left of him,
striped with blood, did not move,
and the women stood back silent,
most of them already smoking
and the others lighting up.

No More Mozart

High to the right a hill of trees,
a fuselage of branches,
reflects German moonlight
like dull armour.
Sieg heil!

Higher still, one moon migrates deathwards,
a white temper between clouds.
To the left, the other slides
undulating on the black
oiled, rippling reservoir.

Can't sleep for Mozart,
and on the winter glass
a shilling's worth of glitter.

The German streets tonight
are soaped in moonlight.
The streets of Germany are clean
like the hands of Lady Macbeth.

Back in bed the eyes close, do not sleep.
Achtung! Achtung!
Someone is breathing nearby,
someone not accounted for.

Now, of course, no more Mozart.
With eyes closed still
the body touches itself, takes stock.
Above the hands the thin wrists
attached to them; and on the wrists
the lampshade material.
Also the little hairs that can be pulled.

The eyes open:
the German earth is made of helmets;
the wind seeps through a deep
frost hole that is somewhere else
carrying the far Jew-sounds of railway trucks.

Nothing is annulled:
the blood vow, the undecorated cry,
someone robbed of his name,
then silence again.

Afterwards:
the needle rests on a record
with nothing on that record turning,
neither sound nor silence,
for it is sleep at last.

There, the fugitive body has arrived
at the stink of nothing.
And twelve million eyes
in six million heads
stare in the same direction.

Outside, the electrician works
inside his cloud, silently,
and the reservoir darkens.

> *Germany, 1970*

The Case

From the ward's far window he stared
through the weighted trees at the tennis court,
its ground red as Devonshire, old rusted blood.
His own had been syringed, drawn off many times,
I learnt from the tall doctor, my colleague,
for sedimentation rates, white cell counts,
haemoglobin content, clotting time,
bleeding time, agglutination tests,
many blood-cultures over many months.
For the patient had been ill many months,
sometimes feeling better, out of bed,
watching the sunlight altering the lawns
or rain in the tennis court. Now, on the grass,
leaves had settled, orange brown yellow,
soaked chemically, dyed in autumn blood.
'Let me speak to your patient then,' I said,
and on the walls the sunlight fused abruptly.
'What's his name?' My colleague had not understood
who knew the man's heart but not the man.
Smiling at rows of beds we walked on
parquet floors, up the ward, and I shook hands
with a shadow. 'Good morning, John,' I said,
reading his name on the temperature chart.

Miracles

Last night, the priest dreamed he quit his church
at midnight, and then saw vividly
a rainbow in the black sky.
I said, every day, you can see
conjunctions equally odd – awake and sane, that is –
a tangerine in the snow, say.
Such things are no more incredible than God.

Such things, said the priest, do not destroy a man,
but seeing a rainbow in the night sky
– awake and sane, that is – why, doctor,
like a gunshot that could destroy a man.
That would not allow him to believe in anything,
neither to praise nor blame. A doctor must believe
in miracles, but I, a priest, dare not.

Then my incurable cancer patient,
the priest, sat up in bed, looked to the window,
and peeled his tangerine, silently.

In the Theatre

(A true incident)

*'Only a local anaesthetic was given because of the blood pressure
problem. The patient, thus, was fully awake throughout the
operation. But in those days – in 1938, in Cardiff, when I was
Lambert Rogers' dresser – they could not locate a brain tumour with
precision. Too much normal brain tissue was destroyed as the
surgeon crudely searched for it, before he felt the resistance of it . . .
all somewhat hit and miss. One operation I shall never forget . . .'*

Dr Wilfred Abse

Sister saying – 'Soon you'll be back in the ward,'
sister thinking – 'Only two more on the list,'
the patient saying – 'Thank you, I feel fine';
small voices, small lies, nothing untoward,
though, soon, he would blink again and again
because of the fingers of Lambert Rogers,
rash as a blind man's, inside his soft brain.

If items of horror can make a man laugh
then laugh at this: one hour later, the growth
still undiscovered, ticking its own wild time;
more brain mashed because of the probe's braille path;
Lambert Rogers desperate, fingering still;
his dresser thinking, 'Christ! Two more on the list,
a cisternal puncture and a neural cyst.'

Then, suddenly, the cracked record in the brain,
a ventriloquist voice that cried, 'You sod,
leave my soul alone, leave my soul alone,' –
the patient's dummy lips moving to that refrain,
the patient's eyes too wide. And, shocked,
Lambert Rogers drawing out the probe
with nurses, students, sister, petrified.

'Leave my soul alone, leave my soul alone,'
that voice so arctic and that cry so odd
had nowhere else to go – till the antique
gramophone wound down and the words began
to blur and slow, '. . . leave . . . my . . . soul . . . alone . . .'
to cease at last when something other died.
And silence matched the silence under snow.

Funland

1 The superintendent

With considerable poise
the superintendent
has been sitting for hours now
at the polished table.

Outside the tall window
all manner of items
have been thundering down
boom boom stagily
the junk of heaven.

A harp with the nerves missing
the somewhat rusty
sheet iron wings of an angel
a small bent tubular hoop
still flickering flickering
like fluorescent lighting
when first switched on
that old tin lizzie banger
Elijah's burnt-out chariot
various other religious hardware
and to cap it all
you may not believe this
a red Edwardian pillar box.

My atheist uncle has been standing
in the corner wrathfully.
Fat Blondie in her pink
transparent nightdress
has been kneeling
on the brown linoleum.
And for some queer reason
our American guest yells
from time to time Mari-*an*
if they give you chewing gum
. . . . CHEW.

Meanwhile the superintendent
a cautious man usually
inclined for instance
to smile in millimetres
has begun to take a great risk.

Calm as usual
masterful as usual
he is drawing the plans of the void
working out its classical proportions.

2 Anybody here seen any Thracians?

The tall handsome man
whom the superintendent
has nicknamed Pythagoras
asked fat Blondie
as she reclined strategically
under the cherry blossom
to join his Society.

The day after that
despite initial fleerings
my uncle also agreed.
The day following another hundred.
Two more weeks everyone
had signed on the dotted line.

There are very few rules.
Members promise to abstain
from swallowing beans. They promise
not to pick up what has fallen
never to stir a fire with an iron
never to eat the heart of animals
never to walk on motorways
never to look in a mirror
that hangs beside a light.
All of us are happy with the rules.

But Pythagoras is not happy.
He wanted to found
a Society not a Religion
and a Society he says
washing his hands with moonlight
in a silver bowl
has to be exclusive.
Therefore someone must be banned.
Who? Who? Tell us Pythagoras.
The Thracians yes the Thracians.

But there are no Thracians among us.
We look left and right wondering
who of us could be a secret Thracian
wondering
who of us would say
with the voice of insurrection
I love you
I love you
not in a bullet proof room
and not with his eyes closed.

Pythagoras also maintains
that Thracians have blue hair and red eyes.
Now all day we loiter near the gates
hoping to encounter someone of this description
so that what is now a Religion
can triumphantly become a Society.

3 The summer conference

On grassy lawns
modern black-garbed priests
and scientists in long white coats
confer and dally.

Soon the superintendent will begin
his arcane disquisition
on the new bizarre secret weapon.
(Psst – the earwigs of R.A.F. Odiham)
Meanwhile I – surprise surprise –
observe something rather remarkable
over there.

Nobody else sees it (near the thornbush)
the coffin rising out of the ground
the old smelly magician himself no less
rising out of the coffin.

He gathers about him his mothy purple cloak.

Daft and drunk with spells
he smiles lopsidedly.
His feet munch on gravel.

He is coming he is coming here
(Hi brighteyes! Hiya brighteyes!)
he is waving that unconvincing
wand he bought in Woolworths.
He has dipped it in a luminous
low-grade oil pool.
Bored with his own act he shouts
JEHOVAH ONE BAAL NIL
Then a lightning flash ha ha
a bit of a rumble of thunder.
Nothing much you understand.
Why should the agéd peacock
stretch his wings?

At once the scientists take off
the priests hurry up
into the sky. They zoom.
They free-wheel high over rooftops
playing guitars;
they perform exquisite
figures of 8
but the old mediocre reprobate
merely shrinks them
then returns to his smelly coffin.
Slowly winking he pulls down the lid
slowly the coffin sinks into the ground.
(Bye brighteyes! Arrivederci brighteyes!)

I wave. I blink.
The thunder has cleared
the summer afternoon is vacated.
As if a cannon had been fired
doves and crows
circle the abandoned green lawns.

4 The poetry reading

Coughing and echo of echoes.
A lofty resonant public place.
It is the assembly hall.
Wooden chairs on wooden planks.
Suddenly he enters suddenly
a hush but for the small
distraction of one chair
squeaking in torment on a plank
then his voice unnatural.

He is an underground vatic poet.
His purple plastic coat is enchanting.
Indeed he is chanting
'Fu-er-uck Fu-er-uck'
with spiritual concentration.
Most of us laugh
because the others are laughing
most of us clap
because the others are clapping.

In the Interval out of focus
in the foyer Mr Poet signs his books.
My atheist uncle asseverates
that opus you read Fuck Fuck –
a most affecting and effective
social protest Mr Poet.

In the ladies' corner though
Marian eyeing the bard
maintains he is a real
sexual messiah
that his poem was not an expletive
but an incitement.
Fat Blondie cannot cease from crying.
She thinks his poem so nostalgic.

Meanwhile the superintendent asks
Mr Poet what is a poem?
The first words Eve spoke to Adam?
The last words Adam spoke to Eve
as they slouched from Paradise?

Mr Poet trembles
he whistles
he shakes his head Oi Oi.
As if his legs were under water
he lifts up and down in slow motion
up and down his heavy feet
he rubs the blood vessels in his eyes
he punches with a steady rhythm
his forehead
and then at last
there is the sound of gritty clockwork
the sound of a great whirring.

He is trying to say something.
His sputum is ostentatious
his voice comes through the long ago.

After the interval
the hall clatters raggedly into silence.
Somewhere else distant
a great black bell is beating
the sound of despair
and then is still.
Cu-er-unt Cu-er-unt chants the poet.
We applaud politely
wonder whether he is telling or asking.
The poet retires a trifle ill.
We can all see that he requires air.

5 Visiting day

The superintendent told us
that last summer on vacation
he saw a blind poet
reading Homer
on a Greek mountainside.

As a result my atheist uncle
has fitted black lenses
into his spectacles.
They are so opaque
he cannot see through them.
He walks around with a white stick.
We shout Copycat Copycat.

In reply his mouth utters
I don't want to see I can't bear to see
any more junk dropping down.
Meanwhile visitors of different sizes
in circumspect clothes in small groups
are departing from the great lawns —
though one alone lags behind and is waving.

She in that blue orgone dress waving
reminds me how I wrote a letter once.
'Love read this though it has little meaning
for by reading this you give me meaning'
I wrote or think I wrote or meant to write
and receiving no reply I heard
the silence.
Now I see a stranger waving.

October evenings are so moody.
A light has gone on
in the superintendent's office.
There are rumours that next week
all of us will be issued
with black specs.

Maybe yes maybe no.

But now the gates have closed
now under the huge unleafy trees
there is nobody.
Father father there is no-one.
We are only middle-aged.
There are too many ghosts already.
We remain behind like evergreens.

6 Autumn in Funland

These blue autumn days
we turn on the water taps.
Morse knockings in the pipes
dark pythagorean
interpretations.

The more we know
the more we journey into ignorance.

All day mysterious aeroplanes
fly over
leaving theurgic vapour trails
dishevelled by the wind
horizontal chalky lines
from some secret script
announcing names perhaps
of those about to die.

Downstairs the superintendent
sullen as a ruined millionaire
says nothing does nothing
stares through the dust-flecked window.
He will not dress a wound even.
He cannot stop a child from crying.

Again at night
shafting through the dark
on the bedroom walls
a veneer wash of radium
remarkably disguised
as simple moonlight.
My vertebral column
is turning into glass.

O remember
the atrocities of the Thracians.
They are deadly cunning.
Our water is polluted.
Our air is polluted.
Soon our orifices will bleed.

These black revolving nights
we are all funambulists.
The stars below us
the cerebellum disordered
we juggle on the edge of the earth
one foot on earth
one foot over the abyss.

7 Death of a superintendent

With considerable poise
in a darkening room
the superintendent sat immobile
for hours at the polished table.
His heart had stopped in the silence
between two beats.

Down with the Thracians.
Down with the Thracians
who think God has blue hair and red eyes.
Down with the bastard Thracians
who somehow killed our superintendent.

Yesterday the morning of the funeral
as instructed by Pythagoras
all members on waking kept their eyes closed
all stared at the blackness
in the back of their eyelids
all heard far away five ancient sounds fading.

Today it's very cold.
Fat Blondie stands inconsolable
in the middle of the goldfish pool.
She will not budge.
The musky waters have amputated her feet.
Both her eyes are crying simultaneously.
She holds her shoes in her right hand
and cries and cries.

Meantime our American guest tries
the sophistry of a song.
The only happiness we know she sings
is the happiness that's gone
and Mr Poet moans like a cello
that's most itself when most melancholy.

To all of this
my atheist uncle responds magnificently.
In his funeral black specs
he will be our new leader.
Look how spitting on his hands first
he climbs the flagpole.
Wild at the very top he shouts
I AM IMMORTAL.

8 Lots of snow

First the skies losing height
then snow raging and the revolution bungled.
Afterwards in the silence
between two snowfalls
we deferred to our leader.
We are but shrubs not tall cedars.

Let Pythagoras be
an example to all Thracian spies
my tyrant uncle cried
retiring to the blackness inside
a fat Edwardian pillar box.

Who's next for the icepick?

Already the severed head of Pythagoras
transforms the flagpole
into a singularly
long white neck.

It has become a god that cannot see
how the sun drips its dilutions
on dumpy snowacres.

And I? I write a letter to someone nameless
in white ink on white paper
to an address unknown.
Oh love I write
surely love was no less
because less uttered or more accepted?

My bowels are made of glass.
The western skies try to rouge the snow.
I goosestep across this junk of heaven
to post my blank envelope.

Slowly night begins in the corner
where two walls meet.
The cold is on the crocus.
Snows mush and melt
and small lights fall from twigs.

Bright argus-eyed the thornbush.

Approaching the pillar box
I hear its slit of darkness screaming.

9 The end of Funland

Uncle stood behind me
when I read Mr Poet's poster
on the billiard cloth
of the noticeboard:
COME TO THE THORNBUSH TONIGHT
HEAR THE VOICES ENTANGLED IN IT
MERLIN'S
MESMER'S
ALL THE UNSTABLE MAGICIANS
YEH YEH
DR BOMBASTUS TOO
FULL SUPPORTING CAST.

Not me I said thank you no
I'm a rational man touch wood.
Mesmer is dead these many years
and his purple cloak in rags.

They are all dead replied uncle
don't you know yet
        all of them dead –
gone where they don't play billiards
haven't you heard the news?

And Elijah the meths drinker
what about Elijah I asked
who used to lie on a parkbench
in bearded sleep – he too?

Of course sneered uncle
smashed smashed years ago like the rest of them
gone with the ravens gone with the lightning.
Why else each springtime
with the opening of a door
no-one's there?

Now at the midnight ritual
we invoke Elijah Merlin Mesmer the best of them
gone with the ravens gone with the lightning
as we stand as usual in concentric circles
around the thornbush.
Something will happen tonight.

Next to me fat Blondie sobs.
Latterly she is much given to sobbing.
The more she sobs the more she suffers.

Suddenly above us
frightful insane
the full moon breaks free from a cloud
stares both ways
and the stars in their stalls tremble.

It enters the black arena aghast
at being seen and by what it can see.
It hoses cold fire over the crowd
over the snowacres of descending
unending slopes.

At last in the distance we hear
the transmigration of souls
like clarinets untranquil played by ghosts
that some fools think to be the wind.

Fat Blondie stops her crying
tilts her face towards me amazed
and holds my hand as if I too were dying.
For a moment I feel as clean as snow.

Do not be misled I say
sometimes Funland can be beautiful
But she takes her hand away.

I can see right through her.
She has become luminous glass.
She is dreaming of the abyss.
We are all dreaming of the abyss
when we forget what we are dreaming of.

But now this so-called moonlight
is changing us all to glass.
We must disperse say goodbye.
We cannot see each other.

Goodbye Blondie goodbye uncle goodbye.

Footprints in the snow
resume slowly up the slope.

They gave me chewing gum so I chewed.

Who's next for the icepick?

Tell me are we ice or are we glass?

Ask Abaris who stroked my gold thigh.

Fu–er–uck fu–er–uck.

Do not wake us. We may die.

Ghosts, Angels, Unicorns

1

Thick curtains closed on a knee-knocking table.
That tall androgynous one, half entranced,
who speaks in an ersatz voice, surely knows
that off-duty ghosts prefer daylight?

Once the ghost of Goethe spoke for them all:
'More light!' Ghosts are the colour of air. They like
lamp-posts that blaze in the streets of morning.
They grin in sunbeams where their small dust shows.

But at night they are hellishly employed
by us: have no leisure to haunt olde inns,
to peacock-screech in Highgate Cemetery
or rap tables. We rarely cease from dreaming.

We moan in sleep and they rush from the wings.
We summon through trap doors a non-union cast.
Weeping they scurry from dream to dream.
We produce them, give them impossible scripts.

2

Most are innocent, shy, will not undress.
They own neither genitals nor pubic hair.
Only the fallen of the hierarchy
make an appearance these secular days.

No longer useful as artists' models,
dismissed by theologians, morale tends
to be low – even high-class angels grumble
as they loiter in our empty churches.

Neutered, they hide when a gothic door opens.
Sudden light blinds them, footsteps deafen,
Welsh hymns stampede their shadows entirely.
Still their stink lingers, cold stone and incense.

But the fallen dare even 10 Downing Street,
astonish, fly through walls for their next trick;
spotlit, enter the dreams of the important,
slowly open their gorgeous Carnaby wings.

3

Were they the first of things to disappear
or just mistranslations from the Hebrew?
Invisible, they graze near stone bridges over streams.
When they drink, sunlight shakes beneath an arch.

They love the forlorn convolvulus flower
of Scotland in which they scratch their flaccid horn.
With eyes closed they think we don't exist.
The gift of sanity no longer theirs.

Their fabulous hoofs make little noise.
They breathe no air and feed upon the dark
no louder than insects that strike the fast
windscreens of cars travelling through summer nights.

Past dawn when there's no more dark to eat
their white horn grows, seeks out a maiden.
Mounted, Sleeping Beauty sighs and stirs,
the gift of sanity no longer hers.

Watching a Cloud

A lacy mobile changing lazily
its animals, unstable faces, till
I imagine an angel, his vapours sailing
asleep at different speeds. My failing:

to see similes, cloud as something other.
Is all inspiration correspondences?
Machinery of cloud and angel both are silent,
both insubstantial. Neither violent.

And, truly, if one shining angel existed
what safer than the camouflage of a cloud?
There's deranged wind up there. God its power!
Let me believe in angels for an hour.

Let sunlight fade on walls and a huge blind
be drawn faster than a horse across this field.
I want to be theological, stare through
raw white angel–fabric at holy bits of blue.

Let long theatrical beams slant down
to stage-strike that hill into religion. Me too!
An angel drifts to the East, its edges burning;
sunny sunlight on stony stone returning.

Three Cars

On the cleared site between tall buildings
three cars, inert, point the same way.
Sunlight clings to their edges, falls off.
If monsters, they seem leucotomized,
do not hear the scattered rhythm of workmen
clanging dull metal nearby – nor beyond,
the obscure grumbling of the background.
Their eyes empty. No flies hover.

Through the afternoon they have waited,
rooftop after rooftop obediently.
Now the last sunlight catches, ignites
excitements of fire and sacrifice.
Two, tumescent, thrill with a deep thrumming.
One chokes. They call each to each. They smash
puffs of blue poison from exhaust pipes.
Such joy – brakes released. They are possessed.

And go wild once past the modest suburbs.
They flee: music crackles, dials glow.
Their six eyes light the country dark.
Half dreaming they descend between black woods
until their red tail lamps disappear.
Out of sight they snarl, overtake each other,
dare not mate. They deposit on the roads
just a little oil in the moonlight.

The Weeping

After I lean from my shadow
to switch on the dark in the lamp,
I sense distant riders
and a disembodied crone-voice rasping,
'Do not weep like a woman
for what you would not fight for as a man.'
Eyes closed before sleep
I think how sleep is a going into exile;
how shadows also
are but cut-out pieces of darkness
exiled from darkness.
(Each summer's day especially,
the diaspora of shadows
awaits the return of night.)

Already, clearly, I hear the advance
of horses, their regular pounding.
Soon two shadows on horseback appear:
one Boabdil, a king long dead,
the other, his scolding mother.
What is dream, what is not dream?
They ride round the corner
of night. They loom near
and become substance. They halt
their horses. They look back
at the alhambra of fable.
(Years since I, a tourist, sauntered
in the alhambra of fable,
read their guidebook story.)

Not the most woeful sound a man may hear,
an exile weeping and weeping.
Yet desolate it is
like a ram's horn blown
in a hushed synagogue,
like Christian bells opening, closing,
like the muezzin heard
even after he has ceased.
Such is the sound this man makes
looking back with clarifying remorse.
No man weeping either,
but a silhouette of a man,
a hunched shadow on horseback,
a homeless shadow weeping.

And I wake up
weeping. I and another both weep
in the darkness, weep in unison.
I wake up. I sit up and stop weeping.
            No-one weeps.

Florida

Not one poem about an animal, she said,
in five, six volumes of poetry,
not one about The Peaceable Kingdom.
An accusation. Was she from the RSPCA?
Your contemporaries have all composed
inspired elegies for expired beasts;
told of salmon flinging themselves up
the sheer waterfall; cold crows,
in black rags, loitering near motorways;
parables of foxes and pheasants,
owls and voles, mice and moles,
cats, bats, pigs, pugs, snails, quails;
so why can't you write one, just one *haiku?*
Oh, I said, Oh! – then wondered if she knew
the story of the starving dowager.

The lady looked as solemn as No.
Well, during the French Revolution,
the dowager, becoming thinner and thinner,
invited other lean aristocrats to dinner.
That night the guests saw (I continued)
slowly roasting on a rotating spit
the dowager's own poodle, Fido,
who proved to be most succulent.
So they made a feast of it.
Afterwards, the dowager sighed,
fingering the pearls about her neck,
sighed and said in noble French,
(I translate) What a damn shame Fido
isn't alive to eat up all those nice
crunchy bones left upon the plate.

My story over, I waited for applause. We'd
never cease from crying, she said,
if *one* insect could relate its misery.
Quite, I said, looking at my paws.
In Florida I saw a floating log
change and chase and swallow up
a barking dog. Hell, I said, an alligator?
A museum snake, too, in Gainesville,
Murder City, I can't forget,
poor black priapus in an empty case
lifting up its head for food not there.
With your gift I'd make a poem out of that.
So try, she said, do try and write
a creature poem and call it *Florida*.
I closed my eyes and she receded.

I thought of tigers and of Blake,
I thought of Fido and his bones.
No, no, she cried, think of Florida.
I saw the hotels of Miami Beach,
I heard waves collapsing ceaselessly.
No no, she said, think again, think
of Florida, its creature kingdom.
Like a TV screen my imagination
lit up to startle the ghost of Blake
with my own eidetic ads for Florida:
first, that black frustrated snake erect,
then two grapefruit inside a brassière.
Open your eyes, the lady screamed, *wake up.*
I'm a poor bifurcated animal, I apologized.
Eagle beagle, bug grub, boar bear.

The Silence of Tudor Evans

Gwen Evans, singer and trainer of singers,
   who, in 1941, warbled
an encore (Trees) at Porthcawl Pavilion
   lay in bed, not half her weight and dying.
Her husband, Tudor, drew the noise of curtains.

Then, in the artificial dark, she whispered,
  'Please send for Professor Mandlebaum.'
She raised her head pleadingly from the pillow,
  her horror-movie eyes thyrotoxic.
'Who?' Tudor asked, remembering, remembering.

Not Mandlebaum, not that renowned professor
  whom Gwen had once met on holiday;
not that lithe ex-Wimbledon tennis player
  and author of *Mediastinal Tumours;*
not that swine Mandlebaum of 1941?

Mandlebaum doodled in his hotel bedroom.
  For years he had been in speechless sloth.
But now for Gwen and old times' sake he, first-class,
  alert, left echoing Paddington for
a darkened sickroom and two large searching eyes.

She sobbed when he gently took her hand in his.
  'But, my dear, why are you crying?'
'Because, Max, you're quite unrecognizable.'
  'I can't scold you for crying about that,'
said Mandlebaum and he, too, began to weep.

They wept together (and Tudor closed his eyes)
  Gwen, singer and trainer of singers,
because she was dying; and he, Mandlebaum,
  ex-physician and ex-tennis player,
because he had become so ugly and so old.

Uncle Isidore

When I observe a toothless ex-violinist,
with more hair than face, sprawled like Karl Marx
on a park seat or slumped, dead or asleep,
in the central heat of a public library
I think of Uncle Isidore – smelly
schnorrer and lemon-tea bolshevik – my foreign
distant relative, not always distant.

Before Auschwitz, Treblinka, he seemed near,
those days of local pogroms, five year programmes,
until I heard him say, 'Master, Master
of the Universe, blessed be your name,
don't you know there's been no rain for years
and your people are thirsty? Have you no shame,
compassion? Don't you care at all?'

And fitting the violin to his beard
he bitterly asked me – no philosopher
but a mere boy – 'What difference between
the silence of God and the silence of men?'
Then, distant, as if in the land of Uz,
the answering sky let fall the beautiful
evening sound of thunder and of serious rain.

That was the first time Uncle went lame,
the first time the doctor came and quit hopelessly.
His right foot raised oddly to his left knee,
some notes wrong, all notes wild, unbalanced,
he played and he played not to that small child
who, big-eyed, listened – but to the Master
of the Universe, blessed be his name.

Tales of Shatz

Meet Rabbi Shatz in his correct black homburg.
The cheder boys call him Ginger.
If taller than 5 foot you're taller than him;
also taller than his father,
grandfather, great grandfather.

Meet Ruth Shatz, née Ruth Pinsky,
short-statured too, straight-backed.
In her stockinged feet
her forehead against his,
her eyes smile into his.
And again on the pillow, later.
Ah those sexy red-headed Pinskys
of Leeds and Warsaw: her mother,
grandmother, great grandmother!

Mrs Shatz resembles Rabbi Shatz's mother.
Rabbi Shatz resembles Mrs Shatz's father.
Strangers mistake them for brother, sister.

At University, Solly Shatz, their morning star,
suddenly secular, all 6 foot of him –
a black-haired centre-forward on Saturdays –
switches studies from Theology to Genetics.

★

A certain matron of Golders Green,
fingering amber beads about her neck,
approaches Rabbi Shatz.
When I was a small child, she thrills,
once, just once, God the Holy One
came through the curtains of my bedroom.
What on earth has he been doing since?

Rabbi Shatz turns, he squints,
he stands on one leg
hoping for the inspiration of a Hillel.
The Holy One, he answers, blessed be He,
has been waiting, waiting patiently,
till you see Him again.

★

Consider the mazzle of Baruch Levy
who changed his name to Barry Lee,
who moved to Esher, Surrey,
who sent his four sons – Matthew, Mark,
Luke and John – to boarding school,
who had his wife's nose fixed,
who, blinking in the Gents,
turned from the writing on the wall
and later, still blinking, joined the golf club.

With new friend, Colonel Owen,
first game out, under vexed clouds,
thunder detonated without rain,
lightning stretched without thunder,
and near the 2nd hole,
where the darker green edged
to the shaved lighter green,
both looked up terrified.
Barbed fire zagged towards them
to strike dead instantly
Mostyn Owen, Barry Lee's opponent.
What luck that Colonel Owen
(as Barry discovered later)
once was known as Moshe Cohen.

Now, continued Rabbi Shatz,
recall how even the sorrows of Job
had a happy ending.

*

Being a religious man Shatz adored riddles.
Who? he asked his impatient wife.

Who like all men came into this world
with little fists closed, departed
with large hands open, yet on walking
over snow and away from sunsets
followed no shadow in front of him,
left no footprint behind him?

You don't know either, opined his wife.
You and your Who? Who?
Are you an owl?
Why do you always pester me with riddles
you don't know the answer of?

Rabbi Shatz for some reason wanted to cry.
If I knew the answers, he whispered,
would my questions still be riddles?
And he tiptoed away, closed the door
so softly behind him
as if on a sleeping dormitory.

Often when listening to music
before a beautiful slow movement
recaptured him, Shatz would blank out,
hear nothing. So now, too, in his lit study
as night rain tilted outside
across dustbins in the lane
he forgot why his lips moved, his body swayed.

Cousin Sidney

Dull as a bat, said my mother
of cousin Sidney in 1940 that time he tried
to break his garden swing, jumping on it,
size 12 shoes – at fifteen the tallest boy
in the class, taller than loping Dan Morgan
when Dan Morgan wore his father's top hat.

Duller than a bat, said my father
when hero Sidney lied about his age
to claim rough khaki, silly ass;
and soon, somewhere near Dunkirk,
some foreign corner was forever Sidney
though uncle would not believe it.

Missing not dead please God, please,
he said, and never bolted the front door,
never string taken from the letter box,
never the hall light off lest his one son
came home through a night of sleet
whistling, We'll meet again.

Aunt crying and raw in the onion air
of the garden (the unswinging empty swing)
her words on a stretched leash
while uncle shouted, Bloody Germans.
And on November 11th, two howls
of silence even after three decades

till last year, their last year,
when uncle and aunt also went missing,
missing alas, so that now strangers
have bolted their door and cut the string
and no-one at all (the hall so dark)
waits up for Sidney, silly ass.

Remembrance Day

Unbuttoned at home, last Sunday afternoon,
Violence snored in the armchair.
This week, eyes moist, our neighbour marches
with the veterans, ready to be televised,
his nationalism narrow as the coffin
in which the invented hero lies.

A vision dies from being too long stared at.
Not only songs of the old wars fade but ghosts
on barbed wire, on a bayonet-blade. Yet still
everything is what it is and another thing
as the black-coated ceremonies begin
under a vapour trail in blue cold skies.

2000 men are taking off their hats. Not one cries
'Folly'; not one from somewhere else
when the hollow trumpets toot and the guns
damply thud. Echo of an echo of an echo
vanishing like that vapour trail.
Whatever happened to you, Dolly?

By nightfall, smoke lurks down pub-lit streets
and cheers! cheers! mademoiselle from 'Armentiers';
and did you die of cancer, Lily Marlene?
You have forgotten, cannot touch the pinewood.
So Violence, beery, lonely as an old tune,
lifts his lapel to smell the paper poppy.

Sons

     Sarcastic sons slam front doors.
   So a far door slams and I think
of Cardiff outskirts where, once, captured acres played
at being small tamed gardens: the concrete way
roads supplanted grass, wild flowers, bosky paths.
Now my son is like that, altering every day.

        I was like that; also like
   those new semis that seemed ashamed,
their naked windows slashed across by whitewash.
At the frontier of Nowhere order and chaos clash.
And who's not lived at the frontier of Nowhere
and being adolescent was both prim and brash?

        Strange a London door should slam
   and I think thus, of Cardiff evenings
trying to rain, of quick dark where raw brick could hide,
could dream of being ruins where ghosts abide.
Do spreading lamps assert themselves too early?
Anglo-Welsh home town, half town half countryside.

        Son, you are like that and I
   love you for it. In adult rooms
the hesitant sense of not belonging quite.
Too soon maturity will civilize your night,
thrust down electric roots, the nameless becoming
consolingly named and your savage darkness bright.

The Test

From a park bench I stare at Centre Point
and dream of Nell, that witty Protestant whore,
while mild clerks and secretaries carnival the grass
and feed the bolder pigeons. They would not ignore
a king's mistress as they now do this derelict
who tries a little dance, solicits me, alas.

Advances, bows, and becomes eerie, becomes a shade
in sunlight. Yes, it's you, old ghost! You lift
your dress and I see nothing. A bottle gleams
in your right hand, an orange balloon in your left.
Oh the irreducible strangeness of things
and the random purposes of dreams.

You thrust your face into mine. What breweries
of oaths! Then you offer another your mouth to kiss
and ask brashly, 'How's your sex-life, lover?'
I know you haunt lunchtime London for more than this
for now you turn your methylated eyes
to Charles II, the statue with a hangover.

Stoned in Soho Square under high trees!
Soon on clacking typewriters secretaries will rout
the day and I shall worry verses such as these,
if not these. And, suddenly, all is inside out:
the king, quelled, has his back to the stews of Soho
and Nell sinks to the grass on arthritic knees,

seems in hell, weeps on all fours, howls at pigeons,
each second becomes less Nell and more a female Caliban.
Oh no ghost she, but suffering flesh, human and unchaste,
and I, fastidious as any office man,
though licensed friend to Caliban, turn away,
turn from her stridency in slow sorrow and distaste.

Nothing

Amnesia. A keyhole. A glass eye.
In sleep, dreams between long blanks;
awake, blanks between brief dreams.
This is the cemetery side of 50.
This is the taste of pure water.
This is the dread revealing nothing.

Beyond the carpeted staircase
the captive evening settles
where the bedroom door is shut
above a bar of brilliance
that becomes, as the landing darkens
darkens, brighter brighter.

The Stethoscope

Through it,
over young women's tense abdomens,
I have heard the sound of creation
and, in a dead man's chest, the silence
 before creation began.

Should I
pray therefore? Hold this instrument in awe
and aloft a procession of banners?
Hang this thing in the interior
 of a cold, mushroom–dark church?

Should I
kneel before it, chant an apophthegm
from a small text? Mimic priest or rabbi,
the swaying noises of religious men?
 Never! Yet I could praise it.

I should
by doing so celebrate my own ears,
by praising them praise speech at midnight
when men become philosophers;
 laughter of the sane and insane;

night cries
of injured creatures, wide–eyed or blind;
moonlight sonatas on a needle;
lovers with doves in their throats; the wind
 travelling from where it began.

White Coat, Purple Coat

White coat and purple coat
   a sleeve from both he sews.
That white is always stained with blood,
   that purple by the rose.

And phantom rose and blood most real
   compose a hybrid style;
white coat and purple coat
   few men can reconcile.

White coat and purple coat
   can each be worn in turn
but in the white a man will freeze
   and in the purple burn.

Joan's

Now that the evening cold is on the crocus
do you feel the ache of something missing?
Snow melts falling, a million small lights fuse

on twigs, fall to pools of darkness on the ground
while, indoors, one note's gone from the piano
– the highest. Listen to the thud of felt.

No, dear, no! Hear rather the other notes
of the right hand. Also the left background.
Their rejoicing, lamenting, candid sound.

Smile Please

(For Stuart Evans)

Young, I'd startle on a dust-free hole in the air,
with electronic or magnesium flash
photograph the other side, reveal reluctant
ghosts or some rare frightful metamorphosis.

I'd catch Leda naked, her face flushed,
her body white like the swan's; or wrathful
Apollo erect and frustrated as Daphne
became less woman, more tree. There were nights

I dreamed a great light picked out momentarily
a unicorn tupping an over-exposed virgin
while other beasts, unknown to man, silently
paced from one secret world to another.

Now the invisible is dark in the blaze of noon
and I'm here and glad beneath a spired church
where over-dressed relatives throw confetti, laugh
and lurch towards a couple enlarged with love.

Older, it's scenes like this that charm me – the disguise
of comedy, blossom of a nettle, a wedding photograph!
And tonight I'll show you the touched-up proof
as new-minted Mr and Mrs kiss and kiss

to prove no developed metamorphosis
can be so wild or as genuine as this.

Bedtime Story

Adam, the first man, my father said, perfect
like the letter A. Blessed be all alephs.
Then my clever question: were there no creatures,

father, before Adam? A long index finger
vertical as a flame to horizontal lips.
Eyes right, eyes left. Whisper of a spy:

yes, unfortunate creatures, angels botched,
badly made, born to be vagrant, born with
the usual amnesia but with little sense

and no sense of direction. They could not
deliver the simplest of messages. . . .
Now, late, I think of that flawed lineage:

of one announcing great news to the wrong Mary
– perhaps it was that unshaved derelict
at the bus station with an empty bottle, muttering –

and here's another in disguise, down at heel,
defeated face white as the salt of Sodom,
veteran among the homeward football crowd

shuffling under hoardings towards nightfall;
and this one supine, over-bearded,
sleeping on a parkbench in his excrement.

Dogs bark and bark at them. They lack pleasure.
They refrigerate the coldness of things.
They stale. They taste the age of their own mouths.

In Casualty rarely cry or grumble.
In wards die with only screens around them.
But now, father, here's *my* bedtime story:

sometimes in the last light of January,
in treeless districts of cities, in a withered
backstreet, their leader can be glimpsed from trains.

He stands motionless in long black overcoat
on spoilt snow and seems like a man again
who yet, father, will outlast the letter Z.

In the Gallery

I

Outside it is snow snow
but here, under the chandelier,
there's no such thing as weather.
Right wall, a horse (not by Géricault);
left, a still life, mainly apples;
between, on the parquet floor, a box
or a coffin which is being opened.

Through a gold-framed mirror
the Director, dressed as if for mourning,
observes the bust
of an unknown lady
by an unknown sculptor
being lifted out of the straw
by a man in overalls.

2

The apples do not rot, the horse will not bolt,
the statue of the lady
cannot breathe one spot
of tissue paper on the mirror.

Her name is forgotten,
the sculptor's name is disputed,
they both have disappeared forever.
They could have been born
in the North or the South.
They have no grave anywhere.

3

Outside it is snow snow
snowing and namelessness is growing.

Yesterday four hoofmarks in the snows
rose and flew away.

They must have been four crows.
Or, maybe, three of them were crows.

A Winter Visit

Now she's ninety I walk through the local park
where, too cold, the usual peacocks do not screech
and neighbouring lights come on before it's dark.

Dare I affirm to her, so agèd and so frail,
that from one pale dot of peacock's sperm
spring forth all the colours of a peacock's tail?

I do. But she like the sibyl says, 'I would die';
then complains, 'This winter I'm half dead, son.'
And because it's true I want to cry.

Yet must not (although only Nothing keeps)
for I inhabit a white coat not a black
even here – and am not qualified to weep.

So I speak of small approximate things,
of how I saw, in the park, four flamingoes
standing, one-leggèd on ice, heads beneath wings.

The Doctor

Guilty, he does not always like his patients.
But here, black fur raised, their yellow-eyed dog
mimics Cerberus, barks barks at the invisible,
so this man's politics, how he may crawl
to superiors, do not matter. A doctor must care
and the wife's on her knees in useless prayer,
the young daughter's like a waterfall.

Quiet, Cerberus! Soon enough you'll have a bone
or two. Now, coughing, the patient expects
the unjudged lie: 'Your symptoms are familiar
and benign' — someone to be cheerfully sure,
to transform tremblings, gigantic unease,
by naming like a pet some small disease
with a known aetiology, certain cure.

So the doctor will and yes he will prescribe
the usual dew from a banana leaf; poppies and
honey too; ten snowflakes or something whiter
from the bole of a tree; the clearest water
ever, melting ice from a mountain lake;
sunlight from waterfall's edge, rainbow smoke;
tears from eyelashes of the daughter.

X-ray

Some prowl sea-beds, some hurtle to a star
and, mother, some obsessed turn over every stone
or open graves to let that starlight in.
There are men who would open anything.

Harvey, the circulation of the blood,
and Freud, the circulation of our dreams,
pried honourably and honoured are
like all explorers. Men who'd open men.

And those others, mother, with diseases
like great streets named after them: Addison,
Parkinson, Hodgkin – physicians who'd arrive
fast and first on any sour death-bed scene.

I am their slowcoach colleague, half afraid,
incurious. As a boy it was so: you know how
my small hand never teased to pieces
an alarm clock or flensed a perished mouse.

And this larger hand's the same. It stretches now
out from a white sleeve to hold up, mother,
your X-ray to the glowing screen. My eyes look
but don't want to; I still don't want to know.

Lunch with a Pathologist

My colleague knows by heart the morbid verse
of facts – the dead weight of a man's liver,
a woman's lungs, a baby's kidneys.

At lunch he recited unforgettably,
'After death, of all soft tissues the brain's
the first to vanish, the uterus the last.'

'Yes,' I said, 'at dawn I've seen silhouettes
hunched in a field against the skyline, each one
feasting, preoccupied, silent as gas.

Partial to women they've stripped women bare
and left behind only the taboo food,
the uterus, inside the skeleton.'

My colleague wiped his mouth with a napkin,
hummed, picked shredded meat from his canines,
said, 'You're a peculiar fellow, Abse.'

Pantomime Diseases

When the fat Prince french-kissed Sleeping Beauty
her eyelids opened wide. She heard applause,
the photographer's shout, wedding-guest laughter.
Poor girl – she married the Prince out of duty
and suffered insomnia ever after.

The lies of Once-upon-a-Time appal.
Cinderella seeing white mice grow into horses
shrank to the wall – an event so ominous
she didn't go to the Armed Forces Ball
but phoned up Alcoholics Anonymous.

Snow White suffered from profound anaemia.
The genie warned, 'Aladdin, you'll go blind,'
when that little lad gleefully rubbed his lamp.
The Babes in the Wood died of pneumonia.
D. Whittington turned back because of cramp.

Shy, in the surgery, Red Riding Hood undressed
– Dr Wolff, the fool, diagnosed Scarlet Fever.
That Jill who tumbled down has wrecked her back,
that Puss-in-Boots has gout and is depressed
and one bare bear gave Goldilocks a heart attack.

When the three Darling children thought they'd fly
to Never-Never Land – the usual trip –
their pinpoint pupils betrayed addiction.
And not hooked by Captain Hook but by
that ponce, Peter Pan! All the rest is fiction.

Of Rabbi Yose

I know little except he would ponder
on the meaning of words in the Torah
till those words became more mysterious
became an astonishment and an error.

'Thou shalt grope at noonday
as the blind gropeth in darkness.'
Soon Yose's eyebrows raised
from that poetry page of curses.
Instead he stared at the adventure
of a white wall and said, 'What difference
to a blind man, noon or midnight?'

All that week, all that month
he puzzled it, '. . . as the blind gropeth . . .',
not reading it as a child would
without obstruction, nor understanding it
as a child could. He thought, too,
of his neighbour, the blind man.

Then coming home late one night
after discussing the Torah with a pupil,
or sickness with a sick man,
one suffering perhaps from the botch
of Egypt, or from emerods, or the scab,

he saw near the darkest foliage
the plumed yellow flame of a torch
moving towards him, held high in the hand
of his neighbour, the blind man.

'Neighbour,' he cried, 'why this torch
since you are blind?' The night waited
for an answer: the wind in a carob tree,
two men, one blind, both bearded, so many
shadows thrown and fleeing from the torch.

'So that others may see me, of course,'
replied the neighbour, 'and save me
from quicksand and rock, from the snake asleep,
from cactus, from thistle and from thornbush,
from the deep potholes in the roadway.'

Year after year, to pupil after pupil,
Yose told of this night-meeting,
told it as parable, told it smiling,
satisfied, with clear-seeing eyes,
and never again pondered the true
lucid meaning of the words:
'Thou shalt grope at noonday
as the blind gropeth in darkness.'

Snake

When the snake bit
Rabbi Hanina ben Dosa
while he was praying

the snake died. (Each day
is attended by surprises
or it is nothing.)

Question: was the bare-footed,
smelly Rabbi more poisonous
than the snake

or so God-adulterated
he'd become immune
to serpent poison?

Oh great-great-great-uncles,
your palms weighing air,
why are you arguing?

Listen, the snake thought
(being old and unwell
and bad-tempered as hell)

Death, where's thy sting?
In short, was just testing:
a snake's last fling.

Yes, the *so-called* snake
was dying anyway, its heart
calcified and as old as Eden.

No, that snake was A1 fit
but while hissing for fun it
clumsily bit its own tongue.

No, Hanina invented that snake;
not for his own sake but for first-
class, religious publicity.

No no, here's the key to it.
Ask: did the Rabbi, later on,
become a jumpy, timid man?

Remember, he who has been bitten
by a snake thereafter becomes
frightened of a rope . . .

Bearded men in darkening rooms
sipping lemon tea and arguing
about the serpent till the moon

of Russia, of Latvia, Lithuania,
Poland, rose above the alien
steeples – centuries of sleep.

Now, tonight, a clean-shaven rabbi
who once studied in Vienna
says snake-venom contains

haemolysins, haemo-
coagulants, protolysins,
cytolysins and neurotoxins

and that even in Hanina
ben Dosa's day a snake was a
snake – unless, of course, it was

a penis, an unruly penis,
making a noise like one pissing
on a mound of fresh hot ashes.

Oh great-great-great-uncles
did you hear him? And are your
handbones weighing moonshine?

Of Itzig and His Dog

To pray for the impossible,
says Itzig, is disgraceful.
I prefer, when I'm on my own,
when I'm only with my dog,
when I can't go out
because of the weather,
because of my shoes,
to talk very intimately to God.

      Itzig, they nag, why do that,
   what's the point of that?
   God never replies surely?

Such ignorance! Am I at the Western Wall?
Am I on spacious Mount Sinai?
Is there a thornbush in this murky room?
God may never say a word,
may never even whisper, Itzig, hullo.

But when I'm talking away
to the right and to the left,
when it's raining outside,
when there's rain on the glass,
when I say please God this
and thank God that,
then God always makes, believe me,
the dog's tail wag.

Jottings

Seekers after truth

Questing, he climbs and climbs, mad-eyed,
far from the dancer and the lyre;
but when he looks up towards the blue
always the mountain grows higher.

Below, distant, the roaring courtiers
rise to their feet – less shocked than irate.
Salome has dropped the seventh veil
and they've discovered there are eight.

Don Juan reports

In the evening she looked like Rachel sweetly
and sweetly said, 'Make yourself feel at home.'
But in the morning she looked like Leah plainly
and I thought I'd rather feel at home at home.

Inspiration

Above Professor Einstein's bed
a portrait of Isaac Newton.
One night Einstein bit an apple and
that portrait fell upon his head.

Transgression

When Eve held in her right hand
the forbidden apple
nothing happened.
So she took a little bite,
a cautious little bite,
and nothing happened.
The great sun shone,
the waterfall fell,
the Paradise birds continued to sing,
so she took another bite
and then another bite,
munch munch munch,
until she'd swallowed the whole damned thing.

Street Scene

(Outside the grocer's, Golders Green Road)

They quarrel, this black-bearded man
and his busy, almost flying wife –
she with her hands, he with proverbs.

'He who never rebukes his son,'
says the bearded man too blandly,
'leads him into delinquency.'

And she who hasn't studied nicely
such studied wisdom, now replies,
'You're a, you're a, you're a donkey.'

Three or four psychiatrists smile
as they pass the greengrocer's shop.
Again, patient, he quotes the Talmud:

'When one suggests you're a donkey
do not fret; only when two speak thus
go buy yourself a saddle.'

But she has thrown appropriate
carrots carrots at his sober head
and one sticks brightly in his beard.

Truce! You have been led into fiction.
Listen! Here comes a violin
and tunes to make a donkey dance.

The bearded man has closed his eyes.
Who's this, disguised as a beggar,
playing a violin without strings?

What music's this, its cold measure?
Who are these, dangling from lamp-posts,
kicking as if under water?

The Power of Prayer

A kind of tune, heart in pilgrimage, yes,
 but reversed thunder as Herbert said?
Herbert was right or we were April fools
last night when we beheld a sign. Behold!
 our Indian neighbour surely praying
since every house across the road was dark
except his own – his bedroom lit by volts,
no doubt, of the thunderstruck eternal.
Why else would those high surprising windows
be raging steadily with sheet lightning?

Herbert, such prayer-power! You'd not credit
 these other, raving, more ancient gods
summoned here by fervent invitation.
How they swarmed in rudely, none so rampant
 as Agni – tawny hair, all gold teeth,
long golden beard – whooping it up crazy
in that attic crackling room, his crimson
snorting horses and his dwarf golden car.
These wild, drunken fire deities! Neighbour,
we thought, oh cease praying do, for God's sake.

And just in case called the bell-mad earthly
    fire brigade whose hoses curved and hushed
so that the gods quit, disguised cleverly,
of course, as tiny butterflies of fire
    or billowing out in cloaks of smoke
and sacred steam. Now no more thunderstorms,
only black debris of last night's party.
And so we godless ones give thanks to God
for godless neighbours this April morning
and for ladders more than rainbows, Herbert.

Night Village

No hare pulls a legless man screaming
into the headlights by his beard.
Driving through the night is not dreaming.

Now it's after two and we are close
to a village asleep which is no
place much. It seems to be all there is.

Here's a few small shops, their unseen glass.
Here's two great dazzling headlights
approaching selfishly. They do not pass.

For at the far corner they are thrown
nowhere. Opposite the Shell garage
closed, suddenly, they're proved to be our own.

This is the brief empty blazing High Street
connecting the one dark road coming in
to the one dark road going out.

And we accelerate, become the speed
of night. Behind us, silence resumes while,
in the mirror, the village lights recede.

No hare pulls a legless man screaming
into the headlights by his beard.
Driving through the night is not dreaming.

Light

Waking from a poorly lit dream
so fast forgetting it
that coming downstairs whistling
I forgot even forgetting.

A letter said, Poets should hold up
lamps in bad light. Why? That others
may see the corpse with placard round
its neck. I could smell gas.

And this for breakfast. The only
permitted whistling seemed to be
the victim's severed windpipe.
Now morning sky dull as ashes.

Forgive me corpse with placard round
your neck. And you, dybbuk, whistling.
Sometimes a man must close his eyes
and ears. So letter to the waste-basket.

Yet, later, rapping the table
without intent, noise in my knuckles,
I discovered the sudden gleam of dead
light from last night's dream.

Less a discovery than a recovery.
Silence and glass in a room —
glass in the window and glass
in the mirror facing that window.

A Note to Donald Davie in Tennessee

Wigged gluttony never your style but will you
                    always eschew,
barbered, the anorexia of fanaticism?
Though we would seldom sign the same petition
or join awkwardly the same shouting march,
neither of us, I hope, would leave through those doors
on the right or on the left marked HYGIENE.

Donald, you're such a northern-rooted man
               you've moved again.
Is home only home away from it? Still poets
jog eagerly, each molehill mistaken
for Parnassus – such energy articulate!
But where's the avant-garde when the procession
runs continuously in a closed circle?

So many open questions to one who prefers
               fugitive ways.
Of course I salute your gifted contradictions –
your two profiles almost the same – like Martin
    Guerre's.
I too am a reluctant puritan, feel uneasy
sometimes as if I travelled without ticket.
Yet here I am in England way out in the centre.

A Sea-Shell for Vernon Watkins

A stage moon and you, too, unreal, unearthed.
Then two shadows athletic down the cliffs
of Pennard near the nightshift of the sea.
You spoke of Yeats and Dylan, your sonorous
pin-ups. I thought, *relentless romantic!*
Darkness stayed in a cave and I lifted
a sea-shell from your shadow when you big-talked
how the dead resume the silence of God.

The bank calls in its debts and all are earthed.
Only one shadow at Pennard today
and listening to another sea-shell I found,
startled, its phantom sea utterly silent –
the shell's cochlea scooped out. Yet appropriate
that small void, that interruption of sound,
for what should be heard in a shell at Pennard
but the stopped breath of a poet who once sang loud?

Others gone also, like you dispensable,
famed names once writ in gold on spines of books
now rarely opened, the young asking, 'Who?'
The beaches of the world should be strewn with such
dumb shells while the immortal sea syllables
in self-love its own name, 'Sea, Sea, Sea, Sea.'
I turn to leave Pennard. This shell is useless.
If I could cry I would but not for you.

Imitations

In this house, in this afternoon room,
my son and I. The other side of glass
snowflakes whitewash the shed roof and the grass
this surprised April. My son is sixteen,
an approximate man. He is my chameleon,
my soft diamond, my deciduous evergreen.

Eyes half closed he listens to pop forgeries
of music – how hard it is to know – and perhaps
dreams of some school Juliet I don't know.
Meanwhile, beyond the bending window,
gusting suddenly, despite a sky half blue,
a blur of white blossom, whiter snow.

And I stare, oh immortal springtime, till
I'm elsewhere and the age my cool son is,
my father alive again (I, his duplicate),
his high breath, my low breath, sticking to the glass
while two white butterflies stumble, held each
to each as if by elastic, and pass.

One Sunday Afternoon

In the courtyard my son with a football.
Here, a woodwormed room fit for suicide.
Locus suspectus. Oakbeams the hack described
where the squire swung two hundred years ago
to become, according to the guidebook,
transparent. Despite leaves falling outside
who can believe in ghosts? Especially in daylight!

So if something stood now against those curtains
to wear their exact design, and if somehow
the window opened slowly like a sign,
how I'd be shaken – wondering whether it
or the colours were being blown apart.
(As in a station, sitting in a carriage,
it seems we move when other trains depart.)

But listen – a small coincidence – a slam
from the hall (the curtains shook) and I am
less rational, more alone, since in my book
not seeing is believing. Hauntings?
Just the hustling wind and a far door bangs
and bangs. So who's unhinged? No snubbed ghost leaving,
no footfall creaks a plank but my own.

All eerie junketings, tall stories of
spooks grieving, the sounds of dread, can go hang –
and this room, too, quiet as language of the roses
or moss upon a wall. I hear nothing
when I hold my breath to hear it breathing.
Instead, from the courtyard, the bounce bounce
of a football and I feel comforted.

In My Fashion

Dear, they said that woman resembled you.
Was that why I went with her, flirted with her,
raised my right hand to her left breast
till I heard the still sad music of humanity?
I complimented you! Why do you object?

Still you shrill, discover everything untrue:
your doppelgänger does not own your birthmarks,
cannot know our blurred nights together.
That music was cheap – a tune on a comb at best,
harsh and grating. Yes, you chasten me

and subdue. Well, that woman was contraband
and compared with you mere counterfeit.
Snow on the apple tree is not apple blossom –
all her colours wrong, approximate,
as in a reproduction of a masterpiece.

Last Words

Splendidly, Shakespeare's heroes,
Shakespeare's heroines, once the spotlight's on,
enact every night, with such grace, their verbose deaths.
Then great plush curtains, then smiling resurrection
to applause – and never their good looks gone.

213

The last recorded words too
of real kings, real queens, all the famous dead,
are but pithy pretences, quotable fictions
composed by anonymous men decades later,
never with ready notebooks at the bed.

Most do not know who they are
when they die or where they are, country or town,
nor which hand on their brow. Some clapped-out actor may
imagine distant clapping, bow, but no real queen
will sigh, 'Give me my robe, put on my crown.'

Death scenes not life-enhancing,
death scenes not beautiful nor with breeding;
yet bravo Sydney Carton, bravo Duc de Chavost
who, euphoric beside the guillotine, turned down
the corner of the page he was reading.

And how would I wish to go?
Not as in opera – that would offend –
nor like a blue-eyed cowboy shot and short of words,
but finger-tapping still our private morse, '. . . love you,'
before the last flowers and flies descend.

Joke

While Freud was tracing the river to its source
he met Itzig unsteadily riding.
'Where are you going?' he asked that wild-eyed rider.
'Don't ask me,' said Itzig. 'Ask the bloody horse.'

Black Flowers

For the summer, I had prepared myself for the summer,
planted summer flowers to welcome friends in my garden.
I hoped for such a display of colour in the summer.

Into my garden a statue trespassed into my garden.
Crazed, he ordered me to turn the black earth over,
saying only black flowers would grow in my garden.

Now summer has come and not one black flower has come
out of the stone-repudiated earth of my garden –
not one flower so much in mourning that friends will not
   come.

And yet, beloved, are these but funeral flowers in my
   garden?
Their colours disguising grief that visitors cannot see?
At midnight, candidly black flowers in my garden?

1948, 1982

Phew!

Do you know that Sumerian proverb
'A man's wife is his destiny'?
But supposing you'd been here,
this most strange of meeting places,
5000 years too early? Or me,
a fraction of a century too late?
No angel with SF wings
would have beckoned,
'This way, madam, this way, sir.'

Have you ever, at a beach,
aimed one small pebble
at another, thrown high, higher?

And though what ends
happily
is never the end,
and though the secret is
there's another secret always,

because this, because that,
because on high the Blessèd
were playing ring-a-ring-o'-roses,
because millions of miles below,
during the Rasoumovsky,
the cellist, pizzicati,
played a comic, wrong note,
you looked to the right, luckily,
I looked to the left, luckily.

Music

Music in the beginning, before the word,
 voyaging of the spheres, their falling transport.
Like phoenix utterance, what Pythagoras heard;
 first hallucinogen, ritual's afterthought.

A place on no map. Hubbub behind high walls
 of Heaven – its bugged secrets filtering out:
numinous hauntings; sacerdotal mating-calls;
 decorous deliriums; an angel's shout.

If God's propaganda, then Devil's disgust,
 plainchant or symphony, carol or fugue;
King Saul's solace, St Cecilia's drug;
 silence's hiding-place – like sunbeams' dust.

Sorrow's aggrandizements more plangent than
  sweet;
 the soul made audible, Time's other beat.

A Scream

That scream from the street erased all content,
that uninspired cry of lunacy
left a vacuum. The ears of our cat

like clown-hats lifted. And silence extended
till this room, at midnight, resumed with one
manic bluebottle tap-tapping the lampshade.

Then you, brave, concerned, pulled the curtains back.
We saw only the emptiness of our street
in lamplight. No blind hunter stumbled by

four times the size of a man. So many
enigmas! That night I dreamt we opened
the little wooden boxes of spikenard,

frankincense, cinnamon, saffron and myrrh;
also that herb from which can rise the antique
S-shaped, slate-coloured smoke to Paradise.

Ceilings

Sleepless, on the bed supine, I wonder
what cranky tenant left this ceiling scorched?
He must have been a giant with a flat iron.
Once, seemingly benign, another ceiling,
fifty shuffled years ago. Under it,
    my mother taught me my name,
    my father taught me the time.

Past bed-time though, poltergeists hurled lights outside,
caused cracks and stains to crawl, go wild, shake loose,
and fall malignantly beside a child
who half-awake, half beneath the bedclothes cried.
The alarm-clock hopped around the room surprised,
    flowers of the wallpaper
    poured forth illicit perfume.

The horror and the fragrance! Even at home
one may become an astonished tourist.
Listen: the oracle and the scalpelled
shadow, mumblings on the landing, almost heard.
Still emissaries from the other world
    seem near but not quite manifest,
    nag the mind like a mislaid word.

A grown man, though, should not rest so menaced,
so two-eyed, in the slow-pacing cuckoo night
of mid-summer, under a whipped ceiling,
to stare and stare again, suspiciously,
as in a zoo, at each primordial
    four-legged stain and serpent-crack
    as now I absurdly do.

Horse

You can't quite
identify it
the long straight road
unsignposted
zipping between hedges
to a scandalously
gorgeous sunset.
As you look closer
shading your eyes
with your right hand
vigilant you'll see
the visitant
the white horse
halfway down it.

Do you remember?
Your father drove the car
the family squabbling
this way years ago
many a time
this Roman road
that's empty now
but for the distant
truant pink horse
with a barely
visible
red shadow
racing towards
the signals of sunset.

War-high in the sky
vapour trails fatten
and you know again
the common sense
of *déjà vu*. Perhaps
someone far from home
should be playing
a mouth organ
a melody slow
and sad and wanton
a tune you've heard
but can't quite say
as the purple horse
surprises the sunset.

And you close your eyes
trying to name it all.
But you recall only
the day's small prose
certain queachy things
what the office said
what the office did
as the sunset goes
as the black horse goes
into the darkness.
And you forget
how from the skin
below your thumbnail
your own moon rises.

In the Holiday Inn

After the party I returned to the hotel.
The room was too hot so I took off my coat.

It was January but I turned down the thermostat.
I took off my shirt but I was still too hot.

I opened the window, it was snowing outside.
Despite all this the air began to simmer.

The room had a pyrexia of unknown origin.
I took off my trousers, I took off my shorts.

This room was a cauldron, this room was tropical.
On the wall, the picture of willows changed

to palm trees. In the mirror I could see the desert.
I stood naked in my socks and juggled

with pomegranates. I offered offerings
that soon became burnt. This was some holiday.

I took off one sock and read the bible.
They were cremating idols, sacrificing oxen.

I could feel the heat of their fiery furnace.
I could hear those pyromaniacs chanting.

I could smell the singed wings of cherubim.
I took off the other sock and began to dance.

Like sand the carpet scalded my twinkling feet.
Steam was coming out of both my ears.

I was King David dancing before the Lord.
Outside it was snowing but inside it was Israel.

I danced six cubits this way, six cubits that.
Now at dawn I'm hotter than the spices of Sheba.

What shall I do? I shall ask my wise son,
Solomon. Where are you Solomon?

You are not yet born, you do not know
how wise you are or that I'm your father

and that I'm dancing and dancing.

Crepuscolo

*Crepuscolo is one of the partly
finished statues by Michelangelo in the Medici
Chapel, San Lorenzo.*

To the grey Sacristy of San Lorenzo
tourists come whispering lest they waken
this self-absorbed statue and it assail
each prying one of them, lest a stone hand
uplift to point and the stone head utter,
slowly turning, 'Wrongdoing and shame prevail!'

Once all drowsy in Carrara. Harmlessly,
unnumbered shadows brooded under the weight
of rock-ledges, lizards hardly animate.
Then certain men came. Still the stone's cry
safe and soundless, still the statue slumbered
in the refuge of the rock's estate.

But, soon, massive slabs were brutally urged
from the mountain – the half-bright, half-stripped bodies
of workmen struggling in dazzle and bone-
white powder of marble, smoking sunlight.
How could they discern the one waking there
or hear stone words in the larynx of the stone?

And later, in Florence? Only the sculptor
heard the statue, almost delivered, crying
'Dear to me is sleep, dearer to be at peace,
in stone, while wrongdoing and shame prevail.
Not to see, not to know, would be a great blessing.'
So the statue pleaded, so the sculptor ceased.

More than four hundred years since they set out
from Carrara, each mile cursed and supervised.
The body in the rock staying young but the hair
turning grey and the face ageing utterly –
its idioplasm fixed, its night-accepting look
despairingly defined in the eyes not there.

Now, this evening, on exercise, three warplanes
dive on Carrara, flee, return, rehearse
radioactive speeds so shamelessly
that, in the x-rayed mountain, another
fifty million statues cower, unhatched,
and not one, stone-enslaved, wanting to be free.

AWOL

Did that spy, that wax golem
in Madame Tussaud's, blink?
Above inverted Kew Bridge
which semblant swan hid
both its beaky heads
under water like a fugitive?

Abruptly tipped off by MI5,
what spirits vacated the fountains
of Trafalgar Square, quit
the fussy trees in Hyde Park?
Who, in Harley St, requested
a prescription for ambrosia?

To answer — Sssh! Sssh! —
is to listen for bare feet
traversing the carpet of a hall;
to hear, in an evening room,
one small needle wakening
a Schubert piano sonata.

Listen, you semiologists!
It's the code of nightfall:
some lit windows, some dark;
fingers without fingerprints;
palms unlined. Forgery
in the sky, fire in the garden.

As if the Dii Majores joked
he was somewhere in London,
one of the sempiternal
30,000, unknown gods
who, after the annual feast,
visibly disappeared: smoke.

Millie's Date

With sedative voices we joke and spar
as white coats struggle around her bed.
Millie's 102, all skull; once her head
was lovely – eyes serious, lips ready to be kissed
at Brixham, in 'the County of Heaven'.
She's outlived three wars and three husbands.
Her only child 'passed over', aged 77.

Sometimes she plucks the life-line in her small
left hand; remarks, 'An itch means money.'
Mostly, though, she's glum or incontinent
with memories. But now, like that immortal
of Cumae who hung in a jar, she cries,
'Let me die, let me die,' – silencing us.
How should we reply? With unfunny science?

Or, 'Not to worry – the Angels of Death
survive forever'? Often I've wondered
if some are disguised as vagrants, assigned
to each of us and programmed to arrive
punctually for their seedy appointments.
So where's Millie's escort, in which doss-house?
Has he lost his way, has he lost his mind?

Millie's quiet now, in a valium doze,
and window by window the building darkens
as lights go home. Outside, I half-expect
a doss-house beggar with a violin
to play, 'Ah, sweet mystery of Life' – some song
like that. Then any passer-by could drop
two coins, as big as eyes, inside his hat.

Case History

'Most Welshmen are worthless,
an inferior breed, doctor.'
He did not know I was Welsh.
Then he praised the architects
of the German death-camps –
did not know I was a Jew.
He called liberals, 'White blacks',
and continued to invent curses.

When I palpated his liver
I felt the soft liver of Goering;
when I lifted my stethoscope
I heard the heartbeats of Himmler;
when I read his encephalograph
I thought, *'Sieg heil, mein Führer.'*

In the clinic's dispensary
red berry of black bryony,
cowbane, deadly nightshade, deathcap.
Yet I prescribed for him
as if he were my brother.

Later that night I must have slept
on my arm: momentarily
my right hand lost its cunning.

Tuberculosis

Not wishing to pronounce the taboo word
I used to write, 'Acid-fast organisms.'
Earlier physicians noted with a quill,
'The animalcules generate their own kind
and kill.' Some lied. Or murmured, 'Phthisis,
King's Evil, Consumption, Koch's Disease.'
But friend of student days, John Roberts, clowned,
'TB I've got. You know what TB signifies?
Totally buggered.' He laughed. His sister cried.
The music of sound is the sound of music.

And what of that other medical student,
that other John, coughing up redness on
a white sheet? 'Bring me the candle, Brown.
That is arterial blood, I cannot be deceived
in that colour. It is my death warrant.'
The cruelty of Diseases! This one, too.
For three centuries, in London, the slow, sad bell.
Helplessly, wide-eyed, one in five died of it.
Doctors prescribed, 'Horse-riding, sir, ride and ride.'
Or diets, rest, mountain air, sea-voyages.

Today, an x-ray on this oblong light
clear that was not clear. No pneumothorax,
no deforming thoracoplasty. No flaw.
The patient nods, accepts it as his right
and is right. Later, alone, I, questing for
old case-histories, open the tight desk-drawer
to smell again Schiller's rotten apples.

In the Old Age Home Where He Says He's Resting

he tree-watches, this autumn, zany Prospero,
ex-stage magician, old star of the lost Empires,
at the window, his powdered face perfect gallows.

Look our own eidolon! Between daft paragraphs
he hums 'Daisy, Daisy', chuckles mildewed jokes
and waits for condescending visitors to laugh.

Like that tree, his mind's half ruined. Again complains
but not of Caliban. 'Son, any child could tell
this place needs renovating, can't you smell the drains?'

Or grumbles: 'Any child could tell they steal my clothes';
suspects the Superintendent's snazzy shirt is his
before switching off to a mouth-gaping doze,

to the bleak mechanism. How molesting it
always is, the last real act. Does Miranda neglect him
now he cannot summon music from the Pit?

Prospero snores on. Ariel is unconfined, free,
and any child could tell but none will tell the child,
'Tis magic, magic, that hath ravished thee.'

A Salute on the Way

(To Peter Porter)

In the Land of late Evening,
miles yet from the bus terminus
where the electric outskirts end
abruptly (far beyond, the Old
Management is about to mend
    the fused stars) I hear you laugh.
    A warm, democratic laugh.

But I remember your 'Alas'
when the needle played the 'sssh' of black
round and round the record's label.
Then the god's thesmothete decreed
(all his aces on the table)
    the game was over – your bill
    the cost of seriousness.

It seems you've often played the lead
in a tragedy translated
by a too cheerful Australian
where the hero, at home, bereaved,
alone and feeling alien,
    takes off unscripted glasses
    quietly, to rub his eyes.

Thus, in the Land of late Evening,
though I hear, now, your candid laugh
more generous than a bridegroom's,
I can guess how, afterwards, you,
like good St Peter, will resume
    the slightly-pained look of one
    about to be crucified

upside-down. Peter-come-lately,
it's your turn to complain of
a *Collected Poems*; of rust
in the morning pelvis; of teeth
touching; of colleagues become dust;
    and nothing to say except
    facts, cats, and thriving heartache,

or who pushed whom and which one fell
(that yellow stain *is* Humpty Dumpty)
so to hell with the Old Management's
jackal-headed, hired psychopomp
whispering of money unspent,
    out there, in the banked darkness:
    'Follow me, follow, follow.'

Friend, let's not hurry. Who believes
these days in a second edition?
May we, unremaindered, go slow,
shadows lengthening between lamp posts
on leafy pavements, or on snow,
    to the very last lamp post
    in the Land of late Evening.

In The Pelican

As a car rushes beneath a railway bridge
and its radio suffers local amnesia
so I'm also afflicted excuse me is that
YOUR glass so sorry with sudden blanks for instance
I've forgotten her name so how can I phone her
look her up in the book though last time in April
when I drove her home February actually
she was an ace she really was I remembered
to remember a mnemonic that would help me
to remember and now I've forgotten THAT
except it had something to do with the colour
of her dress which matched absolutely spot on
the audacious violet colour of her eyes and
YES this should interest you I made the mnemonic
rhyme with one of the old songs the really old songs
like Stormy Weather only it wasn't Stormy
Weather it wasn't Everybody's Doing It
it wasn't Smoke Gets in Your Eyes not Lazybones
not Stardust not Shoe-shine Boy not Whispering Grass
not it's on the tip of my tongue or was it
Thanks for the Memory you know what's his name
used to sing it in tandem with anyway
she was SO desirable and hell I wish I'd
asked her sorry Freud would certainly say something
stupid about how I keep reaching for your glass

A Welcome in the Wolds

Superior people never make long visits. Marianne Moore

First day, Welcome! Welcome! We even ask your
pet centaur — such a sweetie — if he'd like a bed or a
stable
WOULD YOU LIKE A BED OR A STABLE?

First week, we offer you a symphony for a song, a
garden for a daisy. We live to give. You wake to take.

Second week, we are *exhausted* with giving.
Breakfast lunch tea dinner. So much shopping, so
much cooking, so much serving and clearing up. So a
treat, perhaps, at our favourite restaurant?
Your centaur eats like a horse. You *almost* insist on
paying.
This is the beginning of But. This is the beginning
of We don't mind. This is the beginning of Course
not, silly.

Next day your centaur leaves our loo in one
helluva spectacular mess.
Forget it, silly. Forget *it*.

And next week the conclusion of But. For the
foisty centaur phones a friend on Mount Pindus, then
one in the forests of Thessaly, then another in
Famagusta and yet another in *Inner* Mongolia.
For hours.
Naturally he eats the last straw.

So you're for it sweetheart – you and your
phone-mad, full-bottomed, self-centred centaur.
Your finger for a fingernail, your eye for an eyelash.

No matter, when you depart you're smiling, when
you depart we're smiling. Goodbye!
(In the hall, we pretend not to hear your centaur farting.)
Goodbye!
Such a shame you both can't stay,
such a shame your pet must see
his Jungian Analyst.
Goodbye! Goodbye!

Now in the stable – renamed the Hercules Room –
a new sign: NO CENTAURS ALLOWED, NO
NEMEAN LIONS, NO LERNEAN HYDRA,
NO ARCADIAN STAGS, NO
ERYMANTHIAN BOARS, NO CRETAN
BULLS, NO CANNIBAL BIRDS, NO
THREE-HEADED DOGS, ETCETERA,
ETCETERA.

And in our guest-room a little card, beautifully
printed and framed on the wall: YOUR VISIT
GIVES US SO MUCH PLEASURE, IF NOT
YOUR ARRIVAL THEN YOUR
DEPARTURE.

A Translation from the Martian

(For Craig Raine)

Who for the first time on earth saw the object that
earth-men call an and-mirror (sic)
  who incognito picked it up who stared at it whose
eyes widened whose sixth toe curled up
  who cried out delightedly
  'Father. Father.'

Who hid it in his pocket who concealed the object
where his long-dead father lived
  who occasionally gazed at it
  who smiled at it sweetly who spoke to it softly
  'Father. Father.'

Who returned home with it who kept his hand
upon his pocket who did not show the ghost to his
wife
  who became suspicious who came close to smell
him who waited for his sixth toe to fall asleep who
stole the object from his pocket who secretly stared at
it who cried out scornfully
  'Ach. It's only an old woman.'

Who took it to the window who watched it fall in
slow-motion who heard it clatter an hour later
on the red-hard rocks below
  where the and-mirror (sic) broke into moonlight.

Pathetic Fallacies

My dear one is mine as mirrors are lonely. W. H. Auden

Afternoon Mirror

So vain that mirror on the wall.
It waits there and waits there
just to be looked at.

Evening Mirror

Lonely, wishes another mirror
could be brought in, close by, opposite,
that it may reproduce itself.

Night-time Mirror

Suffers from nyctalopia, panics.
Depth charges to its surface. Sleepless,
prays to its own ghost, the window.

Morning Mirror

At last, at last, Visiting Hour.
The portrait gallery is open.
The Director does not seem pleased.

Quests

To reach the other world some sought hemlock
in waste-places: umbels of that small white flower
   still sway at eye-level when the eye is still;

and some, at broad sunset, walked the sea-shore
or prayed for their messiah in a darkening house.
   But gods had human faces and were flawed.

When prying Apion, with eerie conch,
summoned Homer's spirit to ask where he was born
   whose bloody head appeared above the parapet?

Now at this seaport, in its shut museum,
a sculptured satyr on a sculptured sea-horse
   blows only silent zeros through his horn.

And here, out of doors, more abundant silence.
Awesome over the sea, from which no sulking Proteus
   will rise, the candled stars, the unblinking moon.

Who knows? Not me. Secular, I'll never hear
the spheres, their perfect orchestra, or below,
   with joy, old Triton playing out of tune.

The Message

Found in the ruin
this urgent message:
I beg you, kindle
the fire I've prepared
in the secret forest.
Then say the old prayer.

But who can locate
that clandestine forest?
Under which tall tree
should the small fire blaze?
Besides, who can recall
the old words of the prayer?

No matter. Beautiful
the yellowing scroll,
its wild imperative,
its holy message,
that we shall keep safe
in safe or museum.

Encounter at a Greyhound Bus Station

If belief, like heaven, lies beyond the facts
what serpent flies with an ant between its teeth?

asked the over-bearded man with closed eyes.
Who are they who descend when they ascend?

this kabbalist with eyes closed, asked,
Are all men in disguise except those crying?

And what exists in a tree that doesn't exist,
its eggs looted by creatures not yet created?

★

Partial to paradoxes, disliking riddles,
I hummed and I hawed, I advocated

the secrets of lucidity. Then said,
Some talk in their sleep, very few sing.

Abruptly, the unwashed one opened his lids,
rattled one coin inside a tin.

I looked into the splendour of his eyes
and laid my hand upon my mouth.

★

Then he scoffed: You are like the deaf man
who knows nothing of music or of dance

yet blurts out, observing musicians play
and dancers dance – Stupid, how stupid

those who carve the air this way and that,
who blow out their cheeks and make them fat,

who mill about, clutch and maul each other
as if the very earth and all would fall.

★

And what could I, secular, say to that?
That I'm deaf to God but not in combat?

Cool pretensions of reason he'd dismiss
and if I threw stones he'd build a house.

Yet I begged: Dare to reveal, sir, not conceal;
not all, translucent, lose authority.

Fool, he replied, I'm empty, feed my tin,
which I did, of course, when the bus came in.

Exit

As my colleague prepares the syringe
(the drip flees its hour glass)
I feel the depression of Saul,
my mother's right hand grasping still,
her left hand suspiciously still,
and think – Shadow on the wall,
Nothing on the floor – of your
random, katabolic ways:

merciful sometimes, precise, but often
wild as delirium, or like a surgeon
with cataracts grievously unkind
as you are now, as you visit
this old lady – one beloved by me –
as you blunder and exit, moth-blind,
mistaking even the light
on mirrors for open windows;

and as my colleague prepares the syringe
I remember another butchering –
a botched suicide in a circumspect
bed-sitting room, a barely
discernible fake of a girl-corpse,
a marmoreal stillness perfect
except for the closed
plum-skin eyelids trembling;

and as my colleague prepares the syringe
I picture also a victim of war
near a road, a peasant left for dead,
conscious, black-tongued, long-agonized,
able to lift, as my mother can now,
at intervals, her troubled head.
And as my colleague drives the needle in
I want to know the meaning of this:

why the dark thalamus finally
can't be shut down when we sleep
with swift economy? Of that king
and his queen – David and Bathsheba –
the old parable is plain:
out of so much suffering
came forth the other child,
the wise child, the Solomon;

but what will spring from this
unredeemed, needless degradation,
this concentration camp for one?
My colleague forces the plunger down,
squeezes the temgesic out,
the fluid that will numb and stun.
'Shadow on the wall . . .' I call, 'Nothing
on the floor . . . Patron of the Arts!'

And as my colleague extracts the needle
from her vein, the temgesic acts
till the bruised exit's negotiated.
Then how victoriously
you hold the left passive hand
of the dummy in the bed
while I continue uselessly
to hold the other.

Last Visit to 198 Cathedral Road

When, like a burglar, I entered after dark
the ground-floor flat, I don't know why I sat
in the dark, in my father's armchair,
or why, suddenly, with surgeon's pocket-torch
I hosed the objects of the living room
with its freakish light.

Living room, did I say? Dying room, rather.
So much dust, mother! Outraged, the awakened
empty fruit bowl; the four-legged table
in a fright; the vase that yawned hideously;
the pattern that ran up the curtain, took flight
to the long, wriggling, photophobic crack
in the ceiling.

Omnipotent, I returned them to the dark,
sat sightless in the room that was out
of breath and listened, that summer night,
to Nothing.

Not a fly the Z side of the windowpane,
not one, comforting, diminutive sound
when the silence calmed, became profound.

Friends

Since our acorn days we've been friends
    but now at this oak door
I sense you do not wish me well.
    Why so, I cannot tell.

Though red carpet and silver gong
    may welcome us within,
friend, be yourself. Give me your hand.
    Come, this is what we planned.

Bitter as coloquintida
    a green lampshade in the hall
turns the light on your face to bile.
    Friend, turn to me and smile.

I too have felt envy and rage,
    cursed this stranger or that;
with needles in wax, cast a spell,
    damned him or her to hell,

yet never a friend, no, not one
    I would still call a friend.
Now you whom I thought to be loyal
    wish me under the soil.

Apology

I have spoken so much lately
of death and of treachery,
better to have sung the forgotten
other song of Solomon.
Forgive me. I do not believe
the rainbow was invisible
till Noah saw it;
nor was I refreshed
by strange bread in the desert,
spring water in the desert.

The two drab tablets of stone
were two drab tablets of stone,
yet, beloved, this is my heritage;
also music of Solomon's song
on psaltery and dulcimer,
that which is lost but not lost —
like the beautiful rod of Aaron,
the beautiful rod of Aaron
first with its blossom
then with its ripe almonds.

Somewhere

Not because they'd chant a god up with spell,
daft bell, corybantic ceremony,
to hear him speak translated English, badly dubbed,
hardly synchronizing with his lips,

is there a closed room, somewhere, with polished
table, silver tray, glass of soap-bubbles
boiling over. Prettily, these bubbles float
in transparencies of cathedral silence.

They break on soundless objects, on chairs,
on hushed curtains, on ceiling, on walls.

Who wants one coloured bubble not to burst,
a door to open for its triumphant exit?

The Bad Boy of the North-West Coast

Before the grown-ups awake
and the wind blows out the stars
I'll rise and escape from home   —haaya

I'll take clubs for the salmon
carved hooks for the halibut
I'll paddle the great canoe   — haaya

At home they'll cry they'll miss me
I'll hunt for big-breasted girls
I'll give them boiled coloured sweets
and bracelets carved of goat horn
When I'm tall I'll bring them home   — haaya

Then all my leering uncles
will wear their hats of spruce root
will drum and shake their rattles   – haaya

But I'll thrash each one of them
I'll tear off my father's head-dress
I'll marry two girls at once   – haaya

The smaller of the darlings
I'll dress in spotted sealskins
and earrings of abalone shell
the other with bigger breasts
shan't wear anything at all   – haaya, haaya.

American Indian Song

The Young Man and the Lion

(For Tony Whittome)

I

Such thirst, such afternoon heat!
First it would drink then it would eat.
It trod his head into a zwart-storm tree.
          Silently
the young man wept.

The young man who had slept
beside the zwart-storm tree and who
            on waking
in the oven of a lion's mouth
had feigned to be dead.

The lion licked the man's two eyes.
The man felt a stick
pierce that hollow in the back
            of his neck.
So he turned his head a little.

He looked at the lion
            steadfastly.
The lion thought, Is he alive?
And the young man guessing that
it thought he may be alive

settled, would not stir though the stick
sharply was piercing him;
            would not stir
till the lion who first would drink
went three hills away to drink.

Dead, thought the lion. So it went
to drink water from the water.
And the man shifted. And the man ran
            to leave meat-
odour in the zwart-storm tree.

2

'Help!' Zig-zag he ran, open-mouthed.
'Help! Hide me in a hartebeest skin,
save me!' we heard him shout.
'The lion that drank my tears
will surely seek me out.'

Under evening miles of coloured sky
roaring and roaring the lion came
to our village. It would not cease.
The mother of the young man cried,
'Oh kill the lion, kill the beast.'

We hunters raced from the huts,
vultures settled on a wall.
One-eyed we fattened our bows
and aimed at the cheated lion.
The lion was full of arrows.

Strange thing: the lion did not fall,
would not die. What was happening?
We aimed more arrows and some hurled
assagai. Still it would not bleed.
Its soul was in another world.

'Yes,' said the rattle man who knew best.
'That lion by a sorcerer
is charmed or else it would be dead.
Give up the man you're hiding
now the sun is round with blood.'

'No!' the mouth of the mother screamed.
'Not my son, no! I shall go instead.'
And arms outstretched ran out unarmed.
Later we tossed a white-eyed girl child
to the beast. She also was not harmed.

The lion wanted only that man
whose double tears it had drunk.
Roaring it woke the stars in the sky —
they came forth brightly one by one
to watch the lion that would not die.

From the hartebeest skin we pushed him out
and the lion swallowed its roar.
Bristling with arrows, with spears,
it trod the young man, it bit him.
It drank once more his double tears.

Now free to die the lion bled
through its hide blackly. In the dark
it died where the young man lay dead
on the ground. Far from the stars,
the dead man, the dead lion.

   A Bushman Legend (Katkop dialect)

Lesson in Reality (1)

If you see an evil man coming towards you and feel afraid,
make the sign of Shaddai, the sign of the Almighty, with
your right hand and cover your face with it.

Not one man but many
wherever I looked. Here. There.
In every city, every country,

my hand flew to my falling face –
middle fingers, a three-pronged *shin,*
my thumb bent to a *dalet,*
my little finger a crooked *yod.*
The sign of Shaddai.

I grew older:
my forehead spread massively,
my frightened right eye to the right,
my frightened left eye to the left,
and the palm of my hand now too small.

                    T. Carmi (Hebrew)

Lesson in Reality (2)

They held up a stone.
  I said, 'Stone.'
Smiling they said, 'Stone.'

They showed me a tree.
   I said, 'Tree.'
Smiling they said, 'Tree.'

They shed a man's blood.
   I said, 'Blood.'
Smiling they said, 'Paint.'

They shed a man's blood.
   I said, 'Blood.'
Smiling they said, 'Paint.'

   Amir Gilboa (Hebrew)

100 Hats

To balance one hundred hats on my head
100 hats   100 colours
a hundred hats a hundred colours and shades of colour
one hundred hats incandescent with colour

if there were one hundred hats on my head
how I would move with the crowd to the Square
and the people spread open like a fan for me
that I should throw up my hats in the air

if there were one hundred hats on my head
a hundred hats a hundred colours and shades of colour
with the high sun glossing my hundred hats
with the high sun sparkling my hundred colours

how admiringly the people would say to me
100 people   in 100 hats
'hooray' and 'goal' and 'well done' and 'hooray'
and jump with joy with each of my gay flying hats.

Amir Gilboa (Hebrew)

The Merry-Go Round at Night

The roof turns, the brassy merry-go-round crashes
   out music. Gaudy horses gallop tail to snout,
   inhabit the phantasmagoria of light
   substantial as smoke. Then each one vanishes.

Some pull carriages. Some children, frightened, hold tight
   the reins as they arrive and disappear
   chased by a scarlet lion that seems to sneer
   not snarl. And here's a unicorn painted white.

Look! From another world this strange, lit retinue.
   A boy on a steer, whooping, loud as dynamite –
   a sheriff, no doubt, though dressed in sailor-blue.
   And here comes the unicorn painted white.

Faster! The children spell-bound, the animals prance,
    and this is happiness, this no-man's land
    where nothing's forbidden. And hardly a glance
    at parents who smile, who *think* they understand

    as the scarlet lion leaps into the night
    and here comes the unicorn painted white.

                    (A variation of Rilke's 'Das Karussell')

A Note to William Carlos Williams in Heaven

The brown paper
that you described
rolling over

a New Jersey street
and crushed under
tyres of a car

to rise man-sized
in the same wind
down the same road

must have floated
cloud-high above
the Atlantic.

Decades it took
to descend here
in London traffic

more alive than you
to cross with care
at this zebra.

A Wall

in a field in the County of Glamorgan.
You won't find it named in any guidebook.
It lies, plonk, in the middle of rising ground,
forty-four paces long, high as your eyes,
it begins for no reason, ends no place.
No other walls are adjacent to it.
Seemingly unremarkable, it's just there,
stones of different sizes, different greys.

Don't say this wall is useless, that the grass
on the shadow side is much like the other.
It exists for golden lichens to settle,
for butterflies in their obstacle race
chasing each other to the winning post,
for huddling sheep in a slanting rainfall,
for you to say, 'This wall is beautiful.'

The Lesson of Han Fei

'I'm committed,' I gabbled
(in my dream) to the ghost
the colour of water
shaking like water disturbed.
'Committed to difficulty.'
This was in Peking, I think,
a city I have never visited.
He introduced himself
shyly, as Han Fei,
painter-philosopher
of the third century BC.
We discussed, of course,
the water in watercolours
and the art of Art ,
he of the legalist school,
and I, like a fool,
consulting a Chinese-
English phrase book.

This morning, nothing else
of our sweet debate recalled
except his valediction:
'It's hard, sir, hard, hard
to paint a horse or a dog
but easy, damnably easy
to paint a ghost.'
Then bowing gracefully low
he deleted himself,
not even leaving

the smell of a watermark;
and I journeyed on
above an epidemic of ghosts
(shouts from the abyss)
to the Twentieth Century,
my eyes opening to
the water on the windowpane
of a familiar bedroom.

That was hardly an hour ago,
and now, tea-sober, I add,
for the sake of prosaic truth,
(it is still raining)
never have I written a poem
with such damnable ease as this,
'The Lesson of Han Fei'.

Logocracy

The lion hugely roared. 'What? What?'
The barbarians cataleptic, open-mouthed.
Never had they heard one like,
never had they seen one such.

This too-strange obstacle to Rome,
 this testicled adversary unknown.
They parleyed, would not march on.
An omen? A stern god, disguised?

Their leader, word–acrobat
and soul–physician, lied soothingly.
'Only a Roman dog,' he smiled.
'What an amusing bark,' he cried.

So, becalmed, the barbarians
with enthusiastic clubs
beat and beat that manic dog
till its stentorian roaring died.

Of Itzig and the Horse

Now, at dusk, through these binoculars
little Itzig still unsteady
on the galloping animal –
his arms about the horse's neck,
his head behind the horse's head.

And still that bandy fool is talking.
How weirdly innocent he is.
He doesn't know that he is bugged,
that we hear him mutter pleas to God.
Or is he talking to the horse?

The Professor then astounds us.
'That speech, gentlemen, is inhuman.
First, focus your binoculars.
Is it Itzig's mouth that's moving
or is the horse's mouth agape?

'Those hoarse soundings are a horse's,
those fine contractions of the glottis
are indubitably equine:
the expiration before the media
as well as before the tenuis.

'Yes it's odd, dear sirs, quite odd,
but is that horse addressing Itzig
or does the horse converse with God?'
We observe the moon above the hill
and the rider going under it.

The Origin of Music

When I was a medical student
I stole two femurs of a baby
from The Pathology Specimen Room.
Now I keep them in my pocket,
the right femur and the left femur.
Like a boy scout, I'm prepared.
For what can one say to a neighbour
when his wife dies? 'Sorry'?
Or when a friend's sweet child
suffers leukaemia? 'Condolences'?
No, if I should meet either friend
or stricken neighbour in the street
and he should tell me, whisper to me,
his woeful, intimate news,
wordless I take the two small femurs
from out of my pocket sadly
and play them like castanets.

Anti–Clockwise (1)

'Nothing to do with sex, doctor.' Her voice dies.
In the consulting room's firegrate, no fire.
Last summer's dried flowers, sweet lies, nest there.

Now if through her eyes I could slowly pan,
with ophthalmoscope, would I blunderingly
light up single beds in separate bedrooms?

Whispers and sighs. I cannot say, 'What?' again.
So observe her mouth's theatre, how she turns
and turns her wedding ring, anti-clockwise.

Anti-Clockwise (2)

Before breakfast, from my bedroom window,
behold jogging Des, our grey-haired neighbour,
conspicuous in vest and shorts – how he
puffs and blows past our railings.
Rejuvenation therapy, he says.

I think of Abishag the Shunammite,
that most beautiful girl – sheer dynamite –
she ministered to the aged King.
Disaster: he knew her not. Soon was dead.
And Hermann Boerhaave, that Dutch physician,

(13th century) sweet buttery girls failing,
thought he would undo the mortal lock
by placing, instead, two untrousered youths
each side of the prostrate burgomaster.
With what results nobody knows. Don't mock,

only the young don't wish to be younger.
Some, credulous, still receive intramuscular
drug-muck, testicular extracts; some just
eat yoghurt. Once some blithely feasted
on viper-meat or drank youthful blood (cheers!)

from freshly opened veins – and not always
from volunteers. So I suppose it's better
that my cock and cardiac-minded neighbour
this bright and bloody early morning
(his doleful wife still staring at the ceiling)

should run anti-clockwise round the block.

Carnal Knowledge

1

You, student, whistling those elusive bits
of Schubert when phut, phut, phut, throbbed the sky
of London. Listen: the servo-engine cut
and the silence was not the desired silence
between two movements of music. Then
Finale, the Aldwych echo of crunch
and the urgent ambulances loaded
with the fresh dead. You, young, whistled again,
entered King's, climbed the stone-murky steps
to the high and brilliant Dissecting Room
where nameless others, naked on the slabs,
reclined in disgraceful silences – twenty
amazing sculptures waiting to be vandalized.

2

You, corpse, I pried into your bloodless meat
without the morbid curiosity of Vesalius,
did not care that the great Galen was wrong,
Avicenna mistaken, that they had described
the approximate structure of pigs and monkeys
rather than the human body. With scalpel
I dug deep into your stale formaldehyde
unaware of Pope Boniface's decree
but, as instructed, violated you –
the reek of you in my eyes, my nostrils,
clothes, in the kisses of my girlfriends.
You, anonymous. Who were you, mister?

Your thin mouth could not reply, 'Absent, sir,'
or utter with inquisitionary rage.
    Your neck exposed, muscles, nerves, vessels,
a mere coloured plate in some anatomy book;
your right hand, too, dissected, never belonged,
it seemed, to somebody once shockingly alive,
never held, surely, another hand in greeting
or tenderness, never clenched a fist in anger,
never took up a pen to sign an authentic name.
    You, dead man, Thing, each day, each week,
each month, you, slowly decreasing Thing,
visibly losing Divine proportions,
you residue, mere trunk of a man's body,
you, X, legless, armless, headless Thing
that I dissected so casually.
    Then went downstairs to drink wartime coffee.

3

When the hospital priest, Father Jerome,
remarked, 'The Devil made the lower parts
of a man's body, God the upper,'
I said, 'Father, it's the other way round.'
So, the anatomy course over, Jerome,
thanatologist, did not invite me
to the Special Service for the Twenty Dead –
did not say to me, 'Come for the relatives' sake.'
(Surprise, surprise, that they had relatives,
those lifeless-size, innominate creatures.)

Other students accepted, joined in the fake chanting,
organ solemnity, cobwebbed theatre.
And that's all it would have been,
a ceremony propitious and routine,
an obligation forgotten soon enough
had not the strict priest with premeditated rage
called out the Register of the Twenty Dead –
each non-cephalic carcass gloatingly identified
with a local habitation and a name
till one by one, made culpable, the students cried.

4

I did not learn the name of my intimate,
the twentieth sculpture, the one next to the door.
No matter. Now all these years later
I know those twenty sculptures were but one,
the same one duplicated. You.
I hear not Father Jerome but St Jerome cry,
'No, John will be John, Mary will be Mary,'
as if the dead would have ears to hear
the Register on Judgement Day.
    Look, on gravestones many names.
There should be one only. Yours.
No, not even one since you have no name.
In the newspapers' memorial columns
many names. A joke.
On the canvases of masterpieces
the same figure always in disguise. Yours.
Even in the portraits of the old anchorite
fingering a dry skull you are half concealed

lest onlookers should turn away blinded.
In certain music, too, with its sound of loss,
in that Schubert Quintet, for instance,
you are there in the Adagio,
playing the third cello that cannot be heard.

   You are there and there and there, nameless,
and here I am, older by far and nearer,
perplexed, trying to recall what you looked like
before I dissected your face – you, threat,
molesting presence, and I in a white coat
your enemy, in a purple one, your nuncio,
writing this while a winter twig, not you,
scrapes, scrapes the windowpane.

   Soon I shall climb the stairs. Gratefully,
I shall wind up the usual clock at bedtime
(the steam vanishing from the bathroom mirror)
with my hand, my living hand.

A Prescription

Sweet-tempered, pestering
young man of Oxford
juggling with ghazals,
tercets, haikus, tankas,
not to mention villanelles,
terzanelles and rondelets;
conversant with the phonetic
kinships of rhyme, assonance

and consonance; the four
nuances of stress, the three
junctions; forget now
the skeltonic couplet,
the heroic couplet, the split
couplet, the poulter's measure;
speak not of englyn
penfyr, englyn milwr;
but westward hasten
to that rising, lonely ground
between the evening rivers,
the alder-gazing rivers,
Mawddach and Dysynni.

Let it be dark when, alone,
you climb the awful mountain
so that you can count the stars.
Ignore the giant shufflings
behind you – put out that torch! –
the far intermittent cries
of the nocturnal birds,
if birds they are,
their small screams of torture.
Instead, scholar as you are,
remark the old proverb
how the one who ascends
Cadair Idris at night
comes back in dawn's light
lately mad or a great poet.
Meanwhile, I'll wait here
in this dull room of urine-

flask, weighing-machine,
examination-couch, X-ray screen,
for your return (triumphant
or bizarre) patiently.

Arianrhod

Not Arianrhod of Swansea
who could have become a nun,
not cold-flame Arianrhod?
Once, near poppydrowsing corn,
through the cricket weather
consentiently together;
but twice the quarrels after,
dissonances and disorder,
eye-bright denunciations
from theological Arianrhod,
disinclined Arianrhod,
while two rivers were meeting
at Pontneathvaughan.

Night-war came to Swansea
when the kettle was whistling,
Bowdler lay deeper
in Mumbles' graveyard.
Hurdling fire turned to fire
the things it first charred –
both gone Arianrhod's parents
who wailed with the siren,
that ghost-factory siren;
and later stunned Arianrhod
diminished in hospital,
tongue-rotted in hospital,
because their going was hard.

Do names have destinies?
Today in a chronic ward
another Arianrhod, a schizophrene,
picking the frost from her face.
Then back down the landing
heard myself mumbling – Destiny
itself is a man-made name.
Out through the front gate
but still see her standing
on light-iced linoleum,
that used one, Arianrhod,
figure a matchstick,
flame gone without trace.

The Wife of Columbus

After I made love
to the wife of Christopher Columbus
I woke up. Later, over breakfast,
I consulted a map.
Had I not kissed a birthmark
on the soft inside of her right thigh,
a birthmark that resembled
the contours of an island,
familiar but forgotten?
And yet, not necessarily an island.
Error? Columbus thought he'd reached
the spice-rich coast of India.

I have visited, in real daylight,
Columbus, capital of Ohio,
observed Doric buildings
under island-clouds. I have walked
past the Institute of the Blind
questing for something lost, once seen;
also past the Penitentiary
and the Catholic Cathedral
where tall and short women entered,
some hiding their faces
as she did once when the three ships
set sail from the quay at Palos.

Error. I should have journeyed
to a place not on my itinerary –
Columbus, Georgia, perhaps,
and walked all the moody afternoon
beside the Chattahoochee river
searching for a sign;
or Columbus, Indiana, say,
and waited like one asleep
at its junction of railways
for a train of many windows –
with so many sitting skeletons,
so many skulls staring out.

The Ocnophil and the Philobat

Distant the city lights. Now at nightfall
I imagine writ above this ruined door
that opens to a blackness which descends:
'Visitor, discover Nothing here. Endure'.
I dreamed that once and still the words pursue.
I wouldn't go down there if I were you.

I had another dream the other night:
slopes of snow; standing figures cut from ice,
shaped like Henry Moores. They seemed to threaten,
they dragged behind them, blurred and imprecise,
shadows owning a red or purplish hue.
I wouldn't go down there if I were you.

Stone balustrades wind round into the dark
and I drop a stone. So long before it lands.
You remark, 'I'd like to see what lies below,'
and nonchalantly offer me your hand
although the roof above is all askew.
I wouldn't go down there if I . . . *Careful!*

Still you insist and beckon me to come
and childlike shout, 'I dare you. Take a chance,
the more we experience the more we know
and the more we journey into ignorance.'
Agreed, but there are doors I'll not go through.
I wouldn't go down there if I were you.

Musical Moments

1. His Last Piano Lesson (1933)

> *Poet, be seated at the piano*. Wallace Stevens

When, after tea,
(Germany still six million
miles away) Miss Crouch,
the upright piano teacher,
knocks at the front door
the boy's at the back door.
Numbly bored with scales
nimbly scales the wall

and hearing in the park
the pointless cries of children,
joins butter-fingered Jack
and his high-flung tennis ball.

There backslangs
and jabberwocks
swaps acid-drops for bull's-eyes,
Hammond for Hobbs,
and one pocket-aged
PK chewing gum –

till the park-keeper comes
stamping the gravel path,
blowing his whistle,
making the sparrows fly
from their scattered park bench crumbs
(their little noise
the shaking of umbrellas).

Back home, downstairs,
the piano-lid's closed,
a coffin of music.
Their war-faces, their big thumbs.

Exiguous memory:
Remembrance of Crimes Past, 1933,
so few and so many!
On the sideboard,
walnuts in a cut-glass bowl,
and the father raging,
'That's his last piano lesson.'

O joy, Miss dismissed!

Later, only the landing light
under the bedroom door:
no hectoring voices,
no blameless man-sized scarecrow
being thumped down the carpeted stairs
with sovereign impunity

before Sleep's grisly fictions
and forgeries of the world.

2 Outside a Graveyard (1989)

One day, the piano has all the colours of the orchestra;
another day, it brings forth sounds that come from other
worlds. Edwin Fischer

Many nearer than you have gone, too many,
so your going does not touch me deeply,
a one-fingered piano note only
soft as a caress, sounding regret
and then again regret, diminuendo,
spare – hardly a Wagnerian Funeral March;
yet I want to say, 'Sorry, Miss Crouch,'
now that you are dismissed forever.
You were so unassuming and gentle.
If there's a heaven, that's your address.

Once, after the war, I observed you
at a romantic Moiseiwitsch concert,
at Cardiff's plush Empire (so soon after
demolished, replaced by a neon-lit superstore).
You sat thrilled in the stalls, eyes raptly shut –
not in the insanity of prayer but
as if that music was making love to you.

Now I stare at church gargoyles, church spire,
then close my eyes also. Wait! Be patient! Look!
The Assumption of Miss Crouch. There! Up there!
Several hundred feet above the spire,
blessed and sedate in evening dress,
rising slowly above Glamorganshire,
you, old lady, playing the piano –
not an upright piece of furniture either
but a concert-hall, exalted Bechstein,
its one black wing uplifted and beating,
bringing forth sounds from another world,
yes, you and the piano triumphantly rising
between the clouds, higher and higher.

A Footnote Extended

for Thomas Szasz's *Karl Kraus and the Soul Doctors*

Dr Szasz, professor, sir,
I read your book.
I won't make criticisms (I could)
but more attention, please,
for Egon Friedman,
born in Vienna, 1878,
of Jewish parents.

Who, insulted, endured.
Who studied in Berlin,
later in Heidelberg:
studied German
studied philosophy
studied natural science;
did not write a treatise
on the whale,
that hunted mammal
posing as a fish.

But returned to Vienna,
changed his visiting card.
Friedell now, not Friedman.
'Hello Dr Friedell,
you're a mensch, Dr Friedell.
Here's a bowl of wax apples,
here's a vase of paper flowers,
here's margarine in a lordly dish.'

He ignored such tauntings.
Tall, he turned the other cheek,
he converted to Christianity –
defended the Gospel
against Mosaic subversion;
attacked the Jewish Science
of Psychoanalysis,
called its practitioners –
Freud, Abraham, Stekel –
'underground blood-suckers'.

Ah, applause now
for the proselyte
so soon to be successful,
so edgily celebrated
under the probing, chalky
spotlight of cabaret-actor,
writer, critic, author of
Cultural History of the Modern Age.

When the Nazis marched
into Austria –
strange amphigouri
of circumstance –
Friedell, in his bachelor room,
walked towards the long mirror,
saw Friedman approaching.
Whispered Friedman,
screamed FRIEDMAN,
and killed himself.

Of Two Languages

(for Hanoch Bartov)

1

Citizen Dov walking on Mount Carmel
heard Agnon speaking Yiddish to a companion.
'How can you,' complained Dov, 'a five-star scholar,
a great *Hebrew* author, a Nobel prize winner,
prophet amongst men, Solomon amongst Kings,
a genuine, first-class somebody (destined for
a state funeral) how can *you* speak Yiddish?'

'Observe which way we're walking,' replied Agnon.
'Downhill. Downhill, I always speak Yiddish.
Uphill – break forth into singing, ye mountains –
uphill, I speak the language of Isaiah.'

2

Dov, you know Hebrew, you also know Yiddish.
Did you not speak to God in Hebrew
when you spoke to men in Yiddish?

All those used-up, ascetic centuries
of studying the evidence of 22 consonants;
the 23rd would not have destroyed the world.

Now in Hebrew, bellicose, you say, 'Go away.'
Once, softly in Yiddish, you begged, 'Leave me alone.'

Tell me, what's the word for 'mercy' in Hebrew?
In Yiddish, 'mercy' must have many synonyms.

Say now in Yiddish:
'Exile. Pogrom. Wandering. Holocaust.'
Say now in Hebrew:
'Blessed Art Thou O Lord.'

White Balloon

Dear love, Auschwitz made me
more of a Jew than ever Moses did.
But the world's not always with us.
Happiness enters here again tonight
like an unexpected guest
with no memory of the future either;

enters with such an italic emphasis,
jubilant, announcing triumphantly
hey presto and here I am and opening
the June door into our night living room
where under the lampshade's ciliate
an armchair's occupied by a white balloon.
As if there'd been a party.

Of course, Happiness, uninhibited,
will pick it up, his stroking thumb
squeaking a little as he leads us to the hall.
And we shall follow him, too,
when he climbs the lit staircase
towards the landing's darkness,
bouncing bouncing the white balloon
from hand to hand.

It's bedtime; soon we must dream
separately – but what does it matter now
as the white balloon is thrown up high?
Quiet, so quiet, the moon above Masada
and closed, abandoned for the night,
the icecream van at Auschwitz.

A Small Farmhouse Near Brno

What could David Molko do,
in that age of local pogroms
when, forlorn, they appeared in his yard,
those bearded cousins, their wives and children,
who had been fed only on saliva,
the tall and pale and the small and pale,
tearful, destitute, distraught?

'My home's your home,' said Molko,
'the air I breathe will be the air
you breathe. As Ben Azzai promised,
you'll be called by your name,
you'll be given what is yours,
you'll be seated in your place.'

And that first night, near or at the table,
they all sang solemnly, even the children,
to the mournful tune of the Hatikvah:
'Austria, Rumania and Russia too,
all combine to persecute the Jew.'
Then all sat to eat of Molko's meat,
then all stood to drink from Molko's cup.

But it came to pass, nights moonlit or moonless,
they did not sing. Instead, discordances,
small quarrels, nags, weepings, sulks,
gnashing of teeth. For fifteen heads slept
in a farmhouse meant for three or four
and even Molko's equable wife
loudly whispered, 'In the belly
of the fish, Jonah, afflicted,
had more room than we have here.'

Molko, being Molko, consulted the rabbi,
the very old, quivering rabbi,
wise as Shammai, as Hillel even.
He said,
		'Behold, you have chickens, Molko,
white chickens and brown chickens,
in the yard you have chickens.
Therefore I say unto you, Molko,
take them into the house also,
the white and the brown chickens,
those that lay white eggs and
those that lay brown eggs.'

Molko, dubiously, took in the chickens.
And it was worse. Only three nights later
he woke from a nightmare shouting,
'More air, more air.' So, at the hour
when great kings set forth to battle,
Molko once more came unto that rabbi
wise as Shammai, as Hillel even,
who said,
		'Behold, you have four goats, Molko.
I have seen them in your yard.
Though not writ in the chronicles
of the kings of Israel I say unto you
take them in, take the four goats in also.'

Molko stared at the palms of his hands.
But the rabbi told how things bitter
can be made sweet, how the lupine
when diligently boiled, soaked seven times
in water, is made so – as mustard is
or the astringent caper-plant.

So Molko took in the goats,
even the very smelly one he called Buz, the son
of the billy goat Guzi, the son of Toah,
the son of Zuph, the son of Asaph.
And it was worse.

'O Lord hear,' cried Molko's agitated wife
and 'O Lord forgive,' and 'O Lord
hearken and do.' So that after three sabbaths
Molko came once more unto the rabbi
who said,
          'Behold, you have no oxen, Molko,
you have no mules, but you own a donkey.
How manifold are Thy works, O Lord.
Yes, take the donkey who trembles like I do
into your sanctuary. As the Lord liveth,
and as I have two changes of garments,
all will be well, trust me, believe me.'

Thus Molko took into his farmhouse
the donkey that stared at the stinking goats,
that stared at the twelve feathered fowl,
the brown ones and the white ones.
And it was worse.

All fifteen in the little house,
the bearded ones and the unbearded ones,
screamed that it was worse, it was much worse –
like after the desolation of Sodom
and, possibly, Gomorrah.

Now Molko came unto the rabbi
crying, 'Woe, woe,' and his right eye runneth
with water and his left eye runneth
with water. So the rabbi pondered
who had studied all the sages of Israel
and said,
        'Behold, I shall deliver thee.
Take out the donkey, yes, take it out
though like me the donkey feels cold
even in June.'

Molko took the donkey out
into the yard, the uncomprehending donkey.
And it was better. But still
the house quarrelled, gnashed its teeth.
So the rabbi stood on one leg
like Hillel, swaying, vibrating,
till wondrously inspired
he said,
        'Behold, take out the four goats
especially Buz, the son
of the billy goat Guzi, the son of Toah,
the son of Zuph, the son of Asaph.'
And lo, Molko obeyed.
And it was better.

286

But still the house lacked oxygen:
the crying of the children,
the shouting of the women,
the cursing of the bearded ones,
so the rabbi, the very old and wise rabbi
called out,
                'Behold, take out the chickens,
take out the brown ones and the white ones' –
and lo, when the fowl were back in the yard
it was better, oh yes it was better,
and everybody was happy,
so that all now cried out,

'Blessed be the Lord for we are rich,'
and suddenly, it seemed, the little farmhouse
had the height of cedars.
Then they sang near or at the table,
'Austria, Rumania and Russia too,
all combine to persecute the Jew.'

Dog on a Rubbish Tip

This cowering, apocalyptic sky,
light not to be believed,
of impending thunder
and the dark, granular tip
of rubble, charred pulp, tyres
where, improbably, an ancestor
of the totems,
retaining the faculty
of metamorphosis,
chooses the shape of a dog.

Tip, like modern outdoor sculpture,
where a dog hirples for a bone.
The scent teases magnetically,
back and fore, the lodestone-
heavy nose of the dog.
Surprise: has the dog discovered
the bone of a dog?
The wind must have whistled it
to this dishabited
outpost, city's detritus.

The dog, now, master and scholar,
knows that the bone, if bone,
is feigning death. This angers him.
In the dog's grinning mouth
the bone undergoes a seizure.
It cannot resist
its assailant. Its spirit
weeps. In a mania of
paroxysm the dog, exorcist,
shakes it and shakes it.

Ovid should tell this story
of a dog on a rubbish tip.
The sky crackles elsewhere,
the bone is paying its debt
till, at last, dropped, ignored.
Once more dog becomes slave
to the zigzag electric scent
active under the rubble.
Black nose pulled back and fore,
bone changing into a stick.

Magnolia, Golders Hill Park (1)

In the park's walled garden,
beneath the candelabra
of a magnolia tree,
I know a grained wooden seat
that those in distress
should sit upon in silence
when the tree's tonic flowering
is more holy than
a cathedral;
but let no virgin dare
to sit there after dark
lest next morning, profaned,
she be found loitering,
shouting unrestrained, 'Rape! Rape!',
dazed, shivering and insane,
with the tree's white blossom
wildly scattered on the ground,
a little blood-stained.

Magnolia, Golders Hill Park (2)

Now in a dusty July
that will not come again,
I come again to this walled garden
past wooden seats inscribed:
IN MEMORY OF JANE FREEMAN,
IN MEMORY OF DORIS ABBOTS,
IN LOVING MEMORY
OF JOHN CONNELL RIP,
IN FONDEST MEMORY
OF SYLVIA LENNARD
WHO LOVED LIFE,
until I feel myself to be
the word DESOLATION,
wasting the afternoon away,
scribbling these pencilled lines
beneath a magnolia tree
now, itself, so humdrum a green,
so inconspicuous – like Pierre Magnol,
French botanist of the 17th century,
unknown today, his life wiped clean,
except he named this genus of tree:
the magnolia soulangeana,
the umbrella, the sweet bay,
the magnolia grandiflora
or bull bay,
and yulan, the Chinese magnolia.

Ancestor

Black-bearded, white-toothed, lantern-jawed
Antara al-Abse of the sixth century,
remote desert prince, poet of battles,
who answered to no one 'Sir' or 'Lord';
fabulous Bedouin, Maverick and Strong-man,
of white father and black mother, who wrote,
'Half of me comes from the family of Abse,
the other half I defend with my sword.'

I see you approaching the blood-spitting crowd
that backed away from an enormous bull.
'Only Antara can fight this one,' they cried.
If, now, I claim you as my ancestor,
it's not because of your name or fame;
it's because you so temperately sighed,
'Ah yes. But does that bull know I'm Antara?'
And turned away knowing the value of pride.

Staring at a Chandelier

True ancestors of mine,
those in hell, those in heaven,
they're not big wheels
like roaring, war-loving Antara.
They've been allocated
only small, menial jobs,
nothing extraordinary.

In hell,
they're working in the boiler-rooms,
fags scuttling for the great stokers
(dry in the air, plain H_2S);
in hell they're tea-boys for the damned
cigar-smoking disc jockeys
who play otitis media pop music.

In heaven
they're mere storekeepers for the harps
(subtle perfumes of jasmine and ambergris);
in heaven they're brushing down
angel wings or polishing the haloes
– the standard, economy type,
not the real, business-class, gold ones.

How do I know all this,
I, inappropriately dressed
in my one and only suit
(now visibly fatigued, tight-fitting)
kept for formal occasions,
for functions and funerals
of the last twenty-five years?

I had the sense of it in the queue
when the six-foot-four flunkey
shouted, 'Her Highness, the Duchess of This,'
and 'Air Vice-Marshal What,'
and 'General Hyphenated-Why,'
and 'Lord and Lady That,'
then asked me, three times, to repeat my name.

Soon after, I saw it in the predictable
dazzle of a chandelier
high above those ageing folk
gathering in gowns and uniforms
on the red carpet under it
and who, when next I looked,
like the tall flunkey, had vanished.

At Ogmore-by-Sea This August Evening

I think of one who loved this estuary –
my father – who, self-taught, scraped upon
an obstinate violin. Now, in a room
darker than the darkening evening outside,
I choose a solemn record, listen to
a violinist inhabit a Bach partita.
This violinist and violin are unified.

Such power! The music summons night. What more?
It's twenty minutes later into August
before the gaudy sun sinks to Australia.
Now nearer than the promontory paw
and wincing electric of Porthcawl
look! the death-boat black as anthracite,
at its spotlit prow a pale familiar.

Father? Here I am, Father. I see you
jubilantly lit, an ordered carnival.
The tide's in. From Nash Point no foghorns howl.
I'm at your favourite place where once you held
a bending rod and taught me how to bait
the ragworm hooks. Here, Father, here, tonight
we'll catch a bass or two, or dabs, or cod.

Senseless conjuration! I wipe my smile away
for now, lit at the prow, not my father
but his skeleton stands. The spotlight fails,
the occult boat's a smudge while three far lighthouses
converse in dotty exclamation marks.
The ciaccona's over, the record played,
there's nothing but the tumult of the sea.

Brueghel in Naples

About suffering they were never wrong,
The Old Masters . . . W. H. Auden

Ovid would never have guessed how far
and Father's notion about wax melting, bah!
It's ice up there. Freezing.
Soaring and swooping over solitary altitudes
I was breezing along (a record I should think)
when my wings began to moult not melt.
These days, workmanship, I ask you.
Appalling.

There's a mountain down there on fire
and I'm falling, falling away from it.
Phew, the sun's on the horizon
or am I upside down?

Great Bacchus, the sea is rearing
up. Will I drown? My white legs
the last to disappear? (I have no trousers on.)
A little to the left the ploughman,
a little to the right a galleon,
a sailor climbing the rigging,
a fisherman casting his line,
and now I hear a shepherd's dog barking.
I'm that near.

Lest I leave no trace
but a few scattered feathers on the water
show me your face, sailor,
look up, fisherman,
look this way, shepherd,
turn around, ploughman.
Raise the alarm! Launch a boat!

My luck. I'm seen
only by a jackass of an artist
interested in composition, in the green
tinge of the sea, in the aesthetics
of disaster – not in me.

I drown, bubble by bubble,
(Help! Save me!)
while he stands ruthlessly
before the canvas, busy busy,
intent on becoming an Old Master.

The Gates of Paradise

The Baptistery, Florence

Who'd not hesitate before these gilded doors
that Michelangelo, amazed, once described
as gates to grace the entrance to Paradise?

So much we lack, but mere intimate silence
lies within: the coolest shade, the font, the tomb,
and signs, on the marble, of the zodiac.

Besides, sunstruck, the animate street's outside;
so turn these great shut doors around, front to back
that their name, one perfect day, be accurate.

Proposal

Herschel, thrilled, observed a new star
and named it to honour a King;

Dr Livingstone found for his Queen
a waterfall 'smoke which sounded';

and tactful Corot gave Daumier
a house 'to upset the landlord'.

What dare I promise? Mountain signposts
are few and treasures I have none.

Yet come with me, congenial, far,
up the higher indigo roads.

There, memory is imagination
and we may find an eagle's feather.

The Green Field

As soft-eyed lovers for the very first time,
turning out the light for the first time,
blot out all detail, all colours,
and whisper the old code-words, 'Love you',

so those admiring that patch of grass,
there, on the hillside, from this distance
could be in the dark, unconcerned with detail.
'That green field,' they generalize,

though drawing nearer (as to a poem)
they will discover the lies of distance:
rage of different greens. And at the field itself
an unforeseen tapestry of variousness:

sprawl of common weeds and wild flowers,
subtleties of small petals seldom green.

Talking to Blake

I saw a lit candle in sunlight
held by the ghost of William Blake.
He walked by the polluted river, ill-at-ease,
beneath Lambeth's dusty poplar trees.

Then high above Parliament Big Ben struck
and his voice advised as from afar,
'Write visionary lines that give a moral light,
let a poem become a star.'

'Mr Blake,' I replied, 'most poets make
a pale sound now – like a falling snowflake
and the roar of machinery grows
with the automation of the rose.

'Deafened, deafened, are the beautiful Nine
so what you once said remains as true,
the languid strings do scarcely move,
the sound is forc'd, the notes are few.

'All our permutations of despair,
smouldering word-fires without light or heat,
our pursuance of the incomplete,
leave no disturbance in the air.'

'Then,' said he, lowering the candlestick,
(as if to examine a grain of sand)
'the Rose of English Poetry is sick
like England's green and pleasant land.'

Condensation on a Windowpane

I

I want to write something simple,
something simple, few adjectives,
ambiguities disallowed.

Something old-fashioned:
a story of Time perhaps
or, more daringly, of love.

I want to write something simple
that everyone can understand,
something simple as pure water.

But pure water
is H_2O
and that's complicated
like steam, like ice, like clouds.

2

My finger squeaks on glass.
I write JOAN
I write DANNIE.
Imagine! I'm a love-struck
youth again.

I want to say something
without ambiguity.
Imagine! Me, old-age pensioner
wants to say something
to do with love and Time,
love that's simple as water.

But long ago we learnt
water is complicated,
is H_2O, is ice, is steam, is cloud.

Our names on the window
begin to fade.
Slowly, slowly.
They weep as they vanish.

How I Won the Raffle

After I won the raffle with the number 1079,
the Master of Ceremonies asked me why.
'Why did you select that particular number?'

'A man's character is his fate,' I replied,
leaning lazily on a quote as usual.

And suddenly I thought of Schopenhauer's
two last men in the world, two gaunt hermits,
meeting each other in the wilderness,

how an amiable man like Pufendorf
might posulate they'd shake hands;
a Hobbes they'd kill each other;
a Rousseau they'd pass each other by
in terrible silence.

'In short,' said the Master of Ceremonies impatiently,
'you chose 1079 because you had to.'

'In short, I chose 10 because in the old days
ten men used to dance around a new grave.

I chose 7 because those ten men used to dance
around the new grave seven times.'

Also because of the pyramids of Egypt;
the hanging gardens of Babylon;
Diana's Temple at Ephesus;
the great statue of Zeus at Athens;
the Mausoleum at Halicarnassus;
the Colossus of Rhodes;
and the lighthouse of Alexandria.

'I chose 9 because among all numbers
it looks most like a musical note;
nine because of the nine orders of Angels;
nine because of the nine rivers of Hell.'

Also because of Clio with her backward look;
Calliope, stern, staring at her scroll;
Erato, nude, except for her brassière;
Euterpe, eyes closed, flute in mouth;
Terpsichore dancing away, silly one;
Mepomene, arms raised, dagger in hand;
Thalia, mirthless, behind her laughing mask;
Polyhymnia, in sacred robes, orating;
and Urania, dreamy, head amid the stars.

'Sir,' I said,
to the scowling Master of Ceremonies,
'that's why I chose the winning number
1079.'

Between 3 and 4 a.m.

I

Wakeful at 3 a.m.
near the frontiers of Nothing
it's easy, so easy
to imagine (like William Blake)
an archaic angel standing
in a cone of light
not of this world;

easy at the cheating hour
to believe an angel cometh
to touch babies' skulls,
their fontanelles,
deleting the long memory
of generations –
(only prodigies not visited);

easy to conceive angel-light
bright as that sudden,
ordinary window
I saw at midnight
across the road
before the drawing
of its blind.

2

Once, another presence
also nocturnal, oneiric,
secretive, in disguise,
waiting behind
an opening Seder door.

'No,' says the child. 'Gone.'
Framed in that black oblong,
nobody.

(A shadow flies
when a light is shone.)

Was childhood real?
Did a stallion attempt
to mount a mare
painted by Apelles?
Did Greek workmen hear
the exiled statue sob
when carried to
Lord Elgin's ship?

The mystery named
is not the mystery caged.

Even a night-scene
may be an illusion
like an afternoon harbour
viewed through sunglasses,
the light forged
to a moon-tortured sea.

3

I was visited once, once only, elsewhere,
near a lake, near an oak,
near a weeping willow tree and thorn,
one summertime, out of time, in England,
during the cosmic love-making hour
when day and night shyly intermingle,

when day, entranced, does not know what or who
and night, ecstatic, is not itself entirely
till the slow coming of the stars.
But now, weeping willow tree and thorn,
there's only the dread of Nothing.

(Nothing, say the kabbalists
is more real than nothing.)

It's 4 a.m. already and cold
and quiet, quiet as a long
abandoned battlefield.

Late to trawl, net full of holes,
the grounded darkness
for what, naturally, can never be told.

(The unutterable, at best, becomes music.)

No, it's time to hold the silence found
on one side
with the right hand,
the silence on the other
with the left,
then to pull, pull, pull,

till silence tears without a sound.

The Mistake

Come this way through the wooden gate into our garden.
Confront the green tree which once had no identity.
Pluck a leaf. Close your eyes. Smell its acrid odour.
Does it suggest an Oriental dispensary?

One day (after thirteen years) a tree-expert told us
its name: '*Evodia danieli*, without doubt.
From Korea. Odd to find it thriving here in Wales.'
We thanked him. Now we had something to boast about.

When visitors came we offered them a leaf proudly.
'Breathe this in,' we'd urge. 'It's rare as Welsh gold.'
Our olfactory gift, our pagan benediction.
'From Korea,' we'd swank. 'It'll charm away your cold.'

Who, in all of Great Britain, possessed such treasure?
But then came the summer of the drought. Tired of lies
the parched tree suddenly asserted itself, sprouted
ordinary walnuts, shamelessly free of diguise.

A Doctor's Register

And yet God has not said a word!
  'Porphyria's Lover', R. Browning

Half asleep, you recalled a fading list
of girls' sweet names. Now to old women
these names belong – some whom you tumbled and kissed
in summer's twilit lanes or hidden by heather.
You were a youth who never stayed long
for Gwen or for Joyce, for Rita or Ruth
and there were others too, on a lower register.

Then, suddenly, a robust, scolding voice
changed your dream's direction and the weather:
'That much morphia, doctor? Wrong, wrong.'

Surprised to discover your eyes still shut
you wondered which dead patient or what
(whose accusing son and when?) as any
trusted doctor would who did not murder
any pleading one with sovereign impunity.

'I found a thing to do,' said the lover
of Porphyria. *Porphyria?* Awake you add
the other pretty names too: Anuria,
Filaria, Leukaemia, Melanoma,
Sarcoma, Euthanasia, amen.

The Excavation

Absurd those tall stories of tall heroes.
Mine, too. Sixty ells, they said, between
my shoulders! Happy legends of my strength!
Hippy myths of my hair! How I lifted up
a mountain here, a mountain there. Dig, dig:
so little recorded, so many exaggerations.

Three hundred foxes, they said, remember?
Nine, only nine. With a jawbone of an ass,
they said, I topped a thousand men. Dig, dig
for their gritty skulls. I unthatched a mere ten.
Let others boast that I was 'magic',
the rainbow spirit of the Lord about me.

But absent, He, when the whips cracked and I
was led, eyeless, into Dagon's Temple,
heard the hooting crazies on the roof, So many,
the junk Temple collapsed thunderously.
Joke! They thought *I'd* brought the House down –
me, clapped-out circus act, defunct Strong Man.

I was screaming, believe me, I was lost.
Betrayed, betrayed, and so little recorded:
the brevities of a Hebrew scribe only;
a fable for a Milton to embroider;
a picture for a Rubens to paint;
music for the soul of a Saint-Saëns.

Dig, dig, though you will not find Dagon's
stone fish-tail nor the scissors of the sung star
of the Philistines. Who knows the path of that whore
after the Temple, unglued, crashed and crushed?
Did she return to Sorek or raise once more
her aprons in the brothels of Philistia?

Dig, dig. I hear your questing spades muffled,
south of Gaza. Useless. The shifting sands
have buried deeper the graves of all.
Only the wilderness remains, silence
and a jawbone. And marvellous ghosts
people a yellow page of Judges.

History

(To Peter Vansittart)

The last war-horse slaughtered and eaten
long ago. Not a rat, not a crow-crumb
left; the polluted water scarce;
the vile flies settling on the famous
enlarged eyes of skeleton children.

Tonight the moon's open-mouthed. I must
surrender in the morning. But those
cipher tribes out there, those Golden Hordes,
those shit! They'll loot and maim and rape.
What textbook atrocities in the morning?

Now, solitary, my hip-joint aching,
half-lame, I climb the high battlements
carrying a musical instrument.
Why not? What's better? The bedlam of sleep
or the clarities of insomnia?

Look! Below, most fearful perspective:
cloud-fleeing shadows of unending
flatlands; enemy tent after tent
pegged to the unstable moonlight.
You'd think the moon, exposed, would howl.

Besieged city, in some future
history book (aseptic page or footnote)
they'll fable your finale: how
your huck-shouldered, arthritic General,
silhouette on the dark battlements,

played on his pipe a Mongolian song,
an enemy song, played so purely
the Past disrobed, memory made audible,
(sharp as a blade, lonely, most consequent,
that soul-naked melody of the steppes);

how, below, the Mongol soldiers awoke,
listened, leaned on their elbows tamed,
became so utterly homesick, wretched,
so inflamed, that by the cold sweats
of dawnlight, they decamped, departed.

Ha! Such a pleasing, shameless story,
to be told over and over by these
and by those: by propagandists of music;
by descendants of the Mongols.
But, alas, only a scribe's invention.

The truth? I play pianissimo
and not very well. The sleepers
in their tents sleep on, the sentries
hardly stir. I loiter on the battlements.
Stars! Stars! I put away my pipe and weep.

Meurig Dafydd to His Mistress

No word I huffed when Stradling urged the squire
to throw my eulogy on the fire.
The fiddlers laughed. I, snow-silent, proud,
did not melt. But I'm spitless now,
my pearl, my buttercup, my bread-fruit.
I rattle their silver in my pocket.
I have other stanzas for harp and lute,
other gullible lords to flatter.
What do I care for that big-bellied Englishman,
that bugle, that small-beer, that puff-ball,
that dung-odoured sonneteer, John Stradling?

Does he sing perfect metre like Taliesin?
Not that gout-toed, goat-faced manikin.
What does he know of Welsh necks crayoned
by the axe, blood on our feet, our history?
Has he stood pensive at the tomb
of Morien, or Morial, or March?
Wept at any nervous harp, at the gloom
of a dirge for Llywelyn the Last,
or the lament by Lewis Glyn Cothi?
That fungoid, that bunt, that broken-wind,
that bog-bean, can't tell a song from a grunt.

Clean heart, my theology, my sweet-briar,
he'd put our heritage on the fire.
Each night he swigs mead in a safe bed –
never sleeps roofed only by the stars.
At noon, never signs the euphonious nine
sermons of the blackbird. O my lotus,
his lexicon is small compared to mine.
His verses are like standing urine – tepid.
My Welsh stanzas have more heat in them
than the tumbling flames in the fire-place
of the Minstrel Hall of Bewpyr.

Ya

The machine began to hum.
Some blood, they pleaded,
just a little, uncoagulated,
fresh blood, please.
It was springtime, springtime,
the season to open doors.
A pinprick? On the thumb?
They shook their heads.
Hesitant, scrupulous,
sullenly, we detached a finger
– under an anesthetic,
humanely, you understand.
But, afterwards, candid,

they demanded, More blood!
And, ya, after debate
we did amputate a hand:
soft tissues retracted,
joint opened cleanly,
lateral ligaments cut through.
From the wrist.
Better, they said hoarsely,
leaving us discomfited.
What else could we do?
Outside it was springtime, springtime,
the birds' hullabaloo;
the young cried as usual,
not knowing why,
the old because they knew.
So, ya, a whole arm,
almost a perfect job
and without an anaesthetic too.
No wonder they applauded,
their obscene shouts, their keen whistles,
like hosannas from hell.
Allow us this though;
outside it was shifting sunlight,
it was wild bluebells
and, ya, one of us at the window
quoted an English poet–priest:
I do not think I've seen
anything more beautiful
than a bluebell.
I know the beauty
of our Lord by it.

So not till all the women
were released, banished,
did we consent to saw off
a raw foot. Right and left neatly,
our technique swift, improving.
And who could not respond
excitedly – that adrenal flow –
to their rhythmic chanting?
Ya, with both legs wide
then unhinged completely,
oh the powerful voltage
of their male applause
and oh the soulful thrilling
of our National Anthem.
So moving, so very moving,
man it was something.
Fellow scientists,
you can guess
what happened next,
ya, you know
the end of the story.

Beautiful Dead Poets

She spoke of Garcia Lorca murdered;
Hernandez dying in a Franco prison;
Mayakovsky's suicide; how Mandelstam
jumped through the window of a hospital;
Celan and Levi in the Nazi Death Camps.
'Beautiful dead poets, all of them,' said she,
in the delight of enthusiasm.

Behind her, a dark mahogany table
that once had the girth of a lofty tree;
a vase of deep red, drooping lovely things –
aged tulips – untimely ripped from the earth;
and, by the window, a canary caged
because it sang so beautifully.

Ghosting for Mayakovsky

(His suicide note)

I

It's long past one and you must be asleep.
The quiet night's astonished by all the stars.
Why wake you now with a telegram like thunder?

So many thoughts of mystery the night can bring.
Dear love, our love boat's on the rocks. Its sails
wrenched from the mast. No use in adding up the cost,

we're quits; no need to weigh our hearts and hurts
upon the scales. 'No Life without you,' once I said,
and now the strokes of Two thud down like heads from
    blocks.

Our story's over, iconoclast. I'm lost. I'm through.
No need to wake you with a telegram like thunder.
Art's imperative will make these lines come true.

2

Once I drew the Queen of Hearts,
now I'm dealt another card. A club. A two.
Once forbidden love lit up like paper burning
then it charred.

Once with verse of lightning and half in song
I told a daisy and the world
you loved me, you love me not,
and how worthless life unfurled would be
without you – like a single shoe.
I'll not limp along.

I'm shot. I'm through.
Queen of Hearts, O Queen of Hearts,
the imperatives of Art insist,
the lies of Art come true.

Ludic Oblongs

First draw an oblong on an unlined page,
the shape of the page. Now what do you see?

No, Peter, no. Not an upright coffin.
Hardly, it's much too wide for a coffin.

A magician's box. Uh huh. Suppose so.
From which the blonde lady has disappeared

no doubt. What do you think, Melanie? Yes.
A window. Right. What do you see through it?

Snowfields? Acres of snowfields on and on?
Quiet, Mary. It's Melanie's window.

What? A frosted window? C'mon, hardly.
Someone in a bath behind it, perhaps?

Why are you laughing, Peter? What's that, Paul?
Mmm. A cage without bars. The bird has flown.

The bell rang then and I went home happy
till I thought of the real world and its ills.

Oh the uselessness of drawing oblongs
filled with trapped silence or white on white.

Still, here's another, here's its caption:
THE LOST WALK IN THE SAME DIRECTION

Evergreens

'Death? That's for other people,'
homeless Billy Lucas used to say,
sad, sunny-side up, verbal Billy Lucas.

It's winter now in his closed shop-doorway.

He used to roll up his trousers,
dart towards an autumn tree
quicker than a dog-hunted cat
and, at the quivering top, shout out
with spotless joy, 'I am immortal!'

Sometimes he seemed to be
the happiest patient
in that hospital of sorrows.

It's winter now in the grounds of St Ebbas.

The tall deciduous trees have staged
their own phoney funerals
(such morbid, such colourful rehearsals)
and pose for black and white photography.

Who'll cry, 'Long live manic denial,'
esteem the cedar and the yew
and all euphoric Evergreens?

Shmelke

(For A.B.)

Consider the chassidic story of Shmelke
the wise, the celebrated Shmelke of Nikolsburg;
how he, to be honoured among men,
to be word-oiled and garlanded
at the ceremony of ten
dozen uplifted beards,
demanded, first, a room with a mirror.

Before it he stood, head to toe,
solemnly cooing, 'Lo, you are wonderful, Shmelke,
you are generous and compassionate;
you are an eagle above the stars;
you take root downward, bear fruit upward;
you have the energy of broad rivers;
you leap like a hart over the green herb,
over the grass in the field. You are deft,
seemly, and beautiful of countenance.
Shmelke, you are a paragon of virtue;
you are peerless, flawless, humorous,
spiritual like the orange blossom.
You are a saint, Shmelke, holy, holy, holy,
the earth a mere syllable of your glory.'

Those near the portals observing Shmelke,
overhearing Shmelke, were puzzled, disturbed.

'But I was merely preparing myself
by uttering absurdities to the mirror,'
said Shmelke. 'Now I'm ready for your compliments.
Lead me to the platform, let us proceed.'

Cricket Ball

1935, I watched Glamorgan play
especially Slogger Smart, free
from the disgrace of fame, unrenowned,
but the biggest hit with me.

A three-spring flash of willow
and suddenly, the sound of summer
as the thumped ball, alive, would leave
the applauding ground.

Once, hell for leather, it curled
over the workman's crane
in Westgate Street
to crash, they said, through a discreet
Angel Hotel windowpane.

But I, a pre-war boy,
(or someone with my name)
wanted it, that Eden day,
to scoot around the turning world,
to mock physics and gravity,
to rainbow-arch the posh hotel
higher, deranged, on and on, allegro,
(the Taff a gleam of mercury below)
going, going, gone
towards the Caerphilly mountain range.

Vanishings! The years, too, gone like change.
But the travelling Taff seems the same.
It's late. I peer at the failing sky
over Westgate Street
and wait. I smell cut grass.
I shine an apple on my thigh.

Two Photographs

Here's a photograph of grandmother, Annabella.
How slim she appears, how vulnerable. Pretty.
And here's a photograph of grandmother, Doris.
How portly she looks, formidable. Handsome.
Annabella wears a demure black frock with an amber
    brooch.
Doris, a lacy black gown with a string of pearls.
One photo's marked *Ystalyfera* 1880,
the other *Bridgend* 1890.
Both were told to say, 'Cheese'; one, defiant, said 'Chalk!'

Annabella spoke Welsh with a Patagonian accent.
Doris spoke English with a Welsh Valleys' lilt.
Annabella fasted – pious, passive, enjoyed small-talk.
Doris feasted – pacy, pushy, would never pray. Ate pork!
When Annabella told Doris she was damned
indecorous Doris devilishly laughed.
I liked Doris, I liked Annabella,
though Doris was bossy and Annabella daft.
I do not think they liked each other.

Last night I dreamed they stood back to back,
not for the commencement of a duel
but to see who was taller! Now, in these revived
waking hours, my Eau de Cologne grandmothers
with buns of grey hair, of withered rose,
seem illusory, fugitive, like my dream –
or like the dust that secretively flows
in a sudden sunbeam (sieved through leaky curtains)
and disappears when and where that sunbeam goes.

Of two old ladies once uxoriously loved,
what's survived? An amber brooch, a string of pearls,
two photographs. Happening on them, my children's
grandchildren will ask 'Who?' – hardly aware
that if this be not true, I never lived.

In the National Gallery

Each single angel is terrible
        R. M Rilke

Not these, hardly these, not even Piero's
smoothy-faced St Michael, despite big sword
in one hand, nasty snake's head in other;
certainly not the angel Gabriel, mild,
bored with his pose of kneeling and caught again
in the flashlight eyes of wild Fra Lippi:

all said and done, a mere silly, pre-pubertal boy
with a simpering look of 'Gee, you're pregnant!',
overdressed in Sunday-best, peacock's wings
that would not lift him higher than a tree.
And those other angels (God permitting)
who granted impure painters with pure ability

a sitting – how unhappy they appear,
androgynous, holy ones with male names
(designated legends ago, of course, by men)
so tame, surely, that if you cried hosannas,
clapped hands loudly, they'd disappear slowly
back to vast Invisibility.

But that stranger there, so corporeal,
who scowls now at the sweet Virgin of the Rocks,
is he, perhaps, in disguise even to himself,
a descendant of Azazel or Shemhazai?
And others who come in from Trafalgar Square
to be fazed by the fangless spell of moral Art

are they secretly terrible – offspring
of fallen angels and daughters of men:
hair-raising Emim whose glance can stop the heart;
Zamzummim, masters and monsters in war;
Nephilim, called such, since they brought this world
to its still falling fall when they themselves fell?

In the Villa Borghese

The chase. Through the wood, the terror of it.
The choice. Violent love or vegetable asylum.
Still true, sometimes, for uncertain men.
Still true, sometimes, for certain women.
She, with the soul of a nun, chose.

In the Villa Borghese they have become marble.
Millions of days, millions of nights
they pose. He, too, ironically petrified.

With a stethoscope I want to hear
their two hearts beat within the marble.
I want to put a mirror to their mouths.

According to Ovid, she chose. Who cried?
She left him priapic and aching.
Did it rain then? Did he lift his god's leg?

Now I hear, outside, the seminal patter of it
on wide laurel leaves. No matter,
a tree might welcome such fresh drenching.

A feminist victory? Hardly.
True, one more heavy breather denied –
unless, of course, Ovid, pleasing some prim,
some god-loving, soma-loathing priest,
sweetened an older, raunchier story. Lied.

Destinies

(To Francis Celoria)

Sometimes the gods appear to be insane.
So addicted to metamorphosis!
Pity the unloved vulture flying above a roof,
pity the lone eagle settling on a mountain.

Long ago, 'Hail Periphas!' cried the populace
and built a great temple in his honour;
began to call him, 'Overlooker of All'
and at the agora, 'Your Imperial Grace',

offending big-jawed Zeus. His boss-face gorged
with anger – he, flash lord of the thunderbolts,
scandalous incinerator of men –
bridled his ten white horses and charged

over boiling plains towards the Aegean shore
where that afternoon, in sand-dune amour,
Periphas, anastomosing with Phene, sighed,
'Dear one,' while she replied, 'Love evermore!'

Four times unignorable Zeus tapped
the busy bare back of rapt Periphas.
Alas, when Periphas turned he was turned
into a bird, into an eagle that flapped

its wings till Phene, flushed, opened her eyes.
First, surprise. Then appalling cries were heard;
but still she, faithful wife, begged to become
bird also. 'Please Judicious One, All-wise.'

Praised, the god, red-toothed, smiled. Would he concur?
Her nakedness fled and she was covered
with feathers till, heart and head, Phene was
all bird, all sorry-looking vulture.

The sweetness of feminine self-denial!
Are male saints, unmasked, deceiving women?
Other men become wolves to savage other men
so who'd arraign Zeus? Put the gods on trial?

They pester with vipers the sleep of mankind
and, like men, won't forgive those they've injured.
What horrors have they in mind, what transformations
in the zoo of Time to come? To prove unkind?

Sometimes the gods cannot remain aloof
when the populace love a man too much.
Pity the lone eagle flying about a mountain.
Pity the unloved vulture settling on a roof.

Touch Wood

Come, let us praise wood
no longer agrestial.
Not the trillions of coffins
but wood within a living house,
the quietude of an empty bookcase,
the loneliness of scattered chairs –
the metamorphosis
of trees, shrubs, bushes, twigs.
Doors particularly, upstairs, downstairs,
whatever their disposition,
welcoming, half open,
or secretively shut.

It does not matter.
Delightful the craftsmanship
of their lintels,
so comely, so pleasant,
like the repeated oblongs
of windowframes, upstairs, downstairs,
like the serenity of windowsills
that carry vases, flower-pots.
And who could not respond
to the utilitarian elegance
of a wide staircase
rising from a parquet floor?

What a history wood has,
what old echoing stories
in the random museum of the mind:
the gopher ark of Noah
floating high above the mountains;
the huge, staring Trojan horse;
Diogenes's fat barrel;
Horatius's one-way bridge
that fell into the Tiber;
King Arthur's Round Table –
all these relics lost forever
like Jesus's insensate Cross.

Sometimes I think we should construct
in the garden of a living house
an idol of various woods:
head of Lombardy Poplar,
trunk of reliable Oak,
arms of Elm and Pine,
hands of Lime and Plane,
legs of Birch and Beech,
feet of grainy Sycamore
and genitals (of course, discreet)
of musty Fig tree, untidy Fir
and the droopy Weeping Willow.

November nights when we're asleep,
when unbuttoned winds shake the house,
what the spirit of the house
if not the spirit of the forest?
What replies if not primal wood,
dryad-ghost and Daphne-creak,
wild cries of wood awakening?
We, stern-faced as mourners, slumber on,
carry in dream the golden bough
from some black forgotten tree
of the windless underworld
back to the leaf-strewn morning.

Sunflowers

I

Near the back–garden's West wall,
near a synagogue shemozzle of wasps
about michaelmas daisies,
a watchful congregation
of sunflowers in their Sunday best.

Guests of autumn, they too
are enslaved by religion.
Not Jewish or Moslem flowers these;
they pray to the sun,
turn to the South. Obsessed.

II

They do not hear her footsteps.
Choosing, she cuts twelve tall stems.
Held close, the green leaves curl
to the curve of her breast.

Chosen, no apostles these.
Stripped of their leaves, half undressed,
stiff with hubris, their anther-buttons
seem more blatantly manifest.
Twelve glorious atheists
free of the sun's power,
the tyranny of the sun.

The full vase an inflorescence of yellow,
an unashamed zest of yellow,
and merely by admiring we are blessed.

The Curse

On her deathbed my spunky mother
wishing to be left alone, not helped,
cursed me. My hand, mid-air, still as stone.
Her sudden gritty voice jarring and unjust,
a snarling stranger's voice, sister of one
who knew the 32 curses of Leviticus.
The Dukes of Edom would have been amazed,
the Mighty of Moab would have been undone.

That night each man cursed became my brother.

Sunday Night, Monday Morning

Not like the vandal wind outside
upturning trees, wooden park-seats.
Call me subtle, a click half-heard
opening or closing interior doors.

Upstairs, you open both your eyes,
sit up in bed, listening. Only a show
of moon-shadows, vague. Your head sinks
on a sinking pillow. Goodbye clock.

Your sleeping mind has timeless caves
where extinct creatures snore and stir.
I'm home there, like a troglodyte.
I'll find a Cuvier bone for you.

I'll paint dawn murals, you shall dream them.
(Asleep, how much does your breathing weigh?
The air above the clouds is heavier.)
Erotic one, throw high your silver stick.

Ho! A procession: unicorns (how chic),
tall soothsayers, red-gowned Chaldeans
with golden chains about their necks.
They follow you to morning's abattoir.

You draw the curtains back, I'm still here,
your aide-mémoire, your compass-needle,
your master that some call revenant
(quiet as the spider in the bath).

By what I am, know what you do.
You turn tap steam on, exit spider,
(some apocalypse, some aubade)
you wipe the mirror clear of dream.

Thankyou Note

for the unbidden swish of morning curtains
you opened wide – letting sleep-baiting shafts
of sunlight enter to lie down by my side;
for adagio afternoons when you did the punting
(my toiling eyes researched the shifting miles of sky);
for back-garden evenings when you chopped the wood
and I, incomparably, did the grunting;
(a man too good for this world of snarling
is no good for his wife – truth's the safest lie);

for applauding my poetry, O most perceptive spouse;
for the improbable and lunatic, my darling;
for amorous amnesties after rancorous rows
like the sweet-nothing whisperings of a leafy park
after the blatant noise of a city street
(exit booming cannons, enter peaceful ploughs);
for kindnesses the blind side of my night-moods;
for lamps you brought in to devour the dark.

On the Evening Road

A disgrace a man of my age
to have come this far and not to know;
the fields inert with ignorant mist,
the road between, lost, unsignposted.

I may as well sing a little
since no-one's around to hear me,
'The Song of Omega' my father sang
though the words I've mostly forgotten.

I may as well dance a bit, too,
since no-one's around to scold me:
'Disgrace, a man of his age singing
drunkenly – not knowing where he is.'

Now the Caladrius bird lands
as it must, on the road ahead of me
and drops its dung. Turn towards me, bird,
O turn, turn, with your yellow beak.

O Taste and See

Because of a kiss on the forehead
in the long Night's infirmary,
through the red wine let light shine deep.

Because of the thirty-six just men
that so stealthily roam this earth
raise high the glass and do not weep.

Who says the world is not a wedding?
Couples, in their oases, lullabye.
Let glass be full before they sleep.

Toast all that which seems to vanish
like a rainbow stared at, those bright
truant things that will not keep;

and ignorance of the last night
of our lives, its famished breathing.
Then, in the red wine, taste the light.

The Maestro

'I'll portray you with flutes, oboes and harp.'
So Schumann to Clara. As I would you.

Now, in this front room of a tree-repeated street,
I practise mere stumbling tunes. But the maestro
behind me, in the mirror, my discreet double,
plays your music's parables flawlessly,
Schumann-like, strange and tragical and sweet.

At the Albert Hall

Anarchic dissonances first, so that
somewhere else a lonely scarecrow shivers
in a winter field. A mortician's crow
perches on its head. It begins to snow.
They bring the scarecrow indoors. They feed it
with phosphorus so it should glow at night.
A great orchestra's tuning-up is ghost talk.

The wand! Then the sudden tamed silence of
a cemetery. Who dares to blackly cough?
Threatened, the conductor raises both arms,
an invisible gun pressed to his back.
Listen. And they speak of the sweet psalmist
of Israel, of 200 loaves of bread
and of 100 bundles of raisins.

The Musical Express

A boy like you, he had said (1946)
will end up on the Musical Express.

What did that Swiss Cottage refugee,
that graphologist from Vienna
who had escaped the sealed wagons
mean?

I looked at my own handwriting
as if it were a mirror,
saw only a frosted window.

Did he refer merely to symphonic music's
totalitarian finale,
how loudly it accelerates towards silence?

My allegro days are here now:
one morning vast cloudless heaven
unautographed
full of someone else's Forever;
the next, when I blink,
another day, another season,
the stern modesties of a Welsh sky.

You'll end up, son, on the Musical Express.

Rain or shine, days track by so fast now
I can't read the stations' names
that I'm passing through.

One long slanting afternoon,
travelling in the USA when I was young,
first I saw a road sign:

ARCADIA, ONE MILE,
then a line of automobiles
all with headlights on,
coming towards me at mourning pace.

Et in Arcadia ego.

Consider the eyes of baby Hitler
new born, a colourless blue,
that graphologist had said.
Like yours were. Like mine.

Why should I tell you more?
Some touch wood and some stone touches
and a fool is his own informer,
autobiography a form of suicide.

He spoke adagio, that survivor,
– adagio molto espressivo –
and I, so lucky, knew how
the half-sleeping mind has many caves
and a man's country, too, in his fate.

Photograph and White Tulips

A little nearer please. And a little nearer
we move to the window, to the polished table.
Objects become professional: mannequins
preening themselves before an audience. Only
the tulips, self-absorbed, ignore the camera.

All photographs flatter us if we wait
long enough. So we awkwardly Smile please
while long-necked tulips, sinuous out of the vase,
droop over the polished table. They're entranced
by their own puffed and smudgy reflections.

Hold it! Click. Once more! And we smile again
at one who'll be irrevocably absent.
Quick. Be quick! the tulips, like swans, will dip
their heads deep into the polished table
frightening us. Thank you. And we turn thinking

What a fuss! Yet decades later, dice thrown,
we'll hold it, thank you, this fable of gone
youth (was that us?) and we shall smile please
and come a little nearer to the impetuous
once-upon-a-time that can never be twice.

(Never never be twice!) Yet we'll always recall
how white tulips, quick quick, changed into swans
enthralled, drinking from a polished table.
As for those white petals, they'll never fall
in that little black coffin now carrying us.

                              1952, 1995

The Boasts of
Hywel ab Owain Gwynedd

Sunday, skilled in zealous verse I praise the Lord.
Monday, I sing in bed to my busty Nest,
'Such whiteness you are, pear blossom must be jealous.'
Tuesday, scholar Gwladus. Not to love her is a sin.
My couplets she pigeon-coos when I thrust to woo her
till her pale cheeks flush like rosy apple skin.
Wednesday, Generys. Dry old hymns I steal to please her.
Then with passion fruit in season I kneel to ease her.
Thursday, Hunydd, no hesitating lady, she.
One small cherry-englyn and she's my devotee.
Friday, worried Hawis, my epic regular.
She wants no baby, she's gooseberry vehement
till sugared by my poetry of endearment.
Saturday, I score and score. One tidy eulogy
and I'm away – I can't brake – through an orchard
I adore. O sweet riot of efflorescence,
let her name be secret for her husband's sake,
my peach of a woman, my vegetarian diet.

O tongue, lick up juices of the fruit. O teeth
– I've all of mine – be sure my busy tongue keeps quiet.

Lament of Heledd

(based on a fragment of a 9th century Welsh saga poem)

I

I had four brothers. A pike upholds the head
of noble Cynddylan. The corn is red.

I had four brothers. Cynon and Gwiawn
butchered in the straw, their swords not drawn.

Four brothers I had. Vague, hesitant Gwyn
last to fall. Through his neck a javelin.

When will this brute night end? Where shall I go?
Morning's mortuary will be kitchen for the crow.

II

    Cynddylan's Hall is dark tonight.
The stone stairs lead nowhere. No candle glows
behind the lower then the higher windows.

    Cynddylan's Hall is dark tonight
and dark the smoke rising from its ruin.
Slain, slain, are Cynddylan and all our kin.

    Cynddylan's Hall is dark tonight,
its great roof burnt down, I can see the stars.
Curse those Englishmen, their bloody wars.

    Cynddylan's Hall is dark tonight.
No orison is wailed to harp or lute.
O ghost brothers, your sister's destitute.

Cynddylan's Hall is dark tonight,
its silence outrageous. I shall go mad.
I smell skeletons. O blood of my blood.

Cynddylan's Hall is dark tonight.
Should I live on? I am no heroine.
O Cynddylan, Cynon, Gwiawn, and Gwyn.

Welsh Valley Cinema, 1930s

In The Palace of the slums,
from the Saturday night pit,
from an unseen shaft of darkness
I remember it: how, first, a sound
took wing grandly; then the thrill
of a fairground sight — it rose,
lordly stout thing, boasting
a carnival of gaudy-bright,
changing colours while wheezing out
swelling rhonchi of musical asthma.

I hear it still, played with panache
by renowned gent, Cathedral Jones,
'When the Broadway Baby Says Goodnight
it's Early in the Morning' — then he and it
sank to disappear, a dream underground.

Later, those downstairs, gobbing silicosis
(shoeless feet on the mecca carpet),
observed a miracle – the girl next door,
a poor ragged Goldilocks,
dab away her glycerine tears
to kiss cuff-linked Cary Grant
under an elegance of chandeliers.
(No flies on Cary. No holes in *his* socks.)

And still the Woodbine smoke swirled on
in the opium beam of the operator's box
till THE END – of course, upbeat.
Then from The Palace, the damned Fall,
the glum, too silent trooping out
into the trauma of paradox:
the familiar malice of the dreary,
unemployed, gas-lamped street
and the striking of the small Town's clocks.

Sixth-Form Poet

When my acne almost cleared
I fell in love with humankind.
I wanted to requisition Poetry,
a revolution in my mind.

To the barricades not the court,
my gorgeous rage would console.
Though love be blind it sees
with the optic nerve of the soul.

Poetry is written in the brain
but the brain is bathed in blood.
I sang no praises for the King,
I, laureate to Robin Hood.

A Political Prisoner

*Franco could have freed Miguel Hernandez from prison.
How could a shepherd boy used to living in the open air
live seven years in prison. He got TB. His execution was
carried out by Tuberculosis.* Neruda

I

The noise of many knuckles on metal,
we do not hear it.
There is lightning when we are asleep
and thunder that does not speak;
there are guitars without strings
and nightingales with tongues of glass.

Yet even if we imagine it,
the metal sound of bolts shut to,
then feet stamping down echoing corridors,
what can we do who stroll on easy grass,
who smile back at the gracious and the
goodlooking?

Righteous the rhetoric of indignation,
but protesting poems, like the plaster angels,
are impotent. They commit no crimes,
they pass no laws; they grant amnesty
only to those who, in safety, write them.

2

Shepherd from the village, Orihuela,
who, whistling, could mimic different birds,
who, by day, would count the cabra,
by night, from the hills, the straying stars,
you opened your eyelids noiselessly,
found you were sitting, hunched in a cell.
You howled, hurled a bucket at the bars.

Far from the villanelle of nightingales
or the sexual moan in the throat of doves,
they handed you a bible, remarked slyly,
'Poet, feel at home.' Then Hell's Time
seemed to strike its palindrome note
and you knew you would perish in that cell.
'Flesh falls off gradually,
bones collapse suddenly,' you wrote.

347

3

Within the towering walls of every grey jail,
especially at night, the desire to escape
from the clock's small thefts. Maybe for you, too,
once, after lights out, it was carnival time:
drums beating, somersaulting clowns, men on stilts,
each wearing a bull's mask meant to chill,
and lewd codpieces of unnatural size.
Then the coloured carts and their pretty lanterns,
marching girls in skimpy skirts, bare lifting thighs,
fire-swallowers and those with a juggling skill.

Surely they came, moving pictures, floating
like pointillist dust in substantial moonbeams,
through your cramped cell – though vanishing at dawn
when all the birds that ever were, near and remote,
did not sweetly sing or corvine croak; but coughed,
as you did, spills of bacilli and blood.

The stinking vultures! The pterodactyls!

'You threw me a lemon, it was sour,' you wrote.

1961–1994

C'est la Vie Politique

When promised
a subtle perfume,
tactful dilutions
of musk, civet, ambergris,

expect 'a human error',
a veritable gasworks.
Dry in the polluted air
plain H_2S.

When promised
a hundred-piece orchestra –
Berlioz, Mahler –
a tune on a comb.

When a Queen's diamond,
a snail's shell;
when a King's golden crown,
a funny paper hat.

Consider Mr Maltby,
fancy tailor, who agreed
a suicide pact
with his wife.

She did not falter;
he was unable.
He propped her up
naked in the bath.

Night after night
brought lit candles
into that bathroom
where he quietly dined,

faithfully choosing
her favourite dishes,
fish mainly – turbot, trout –
gently removing the bones.

Refugee

What is the name of your country?
  Its frontiers keep changing.
What is the Capital of your country?
  The town where blood issued
  through the cold and hot water taps.
What is your National Anthem?
  The ancient fugue of screams.
Who are your compatriots?
  The crippled, the groping blinded,
  the wan dead not yet in their dungeons.
Who is your leader?
  Death's trumpet-tongued fool.
What is the name of your son?
  Despair.
What is the name of your daughter?
  Derangement.
Why is your husband not with you?
  He raised high the pleading
  white flag of surrender.

A Heritage

A heritage of a sort.
A heritage of comradeship and suffocation.

The bawling pit-hooter and the god's
explosive foray, vengeance, before retreating
to his throne of sulphur.

Now this black-robed god of fossils
and funerals,
petrifier of underground forests
and flowers,
emerges with his grim retinue
past a pony's skeleton, past human skulls,
into his half-propped up, empty, carbon colony.

Above, on the brutalized,
unstitched side of a Welsh mountain,
it has to be someone from somewhere else
who will sing solo

not of the marasmus of the Valleys,
the pit-wheels that do not turn,
the pump-house abandoned;

nor of how, after a half-mile fall
regiments of miners' lamps
no longer, midge-like,
rise and slip and bob.

Only someone uncommitted,
someone from somewhere else,
panorama-high on a coal-tip
may jubilantly laud
the re-entry of the exiled god
into his shadowless kingdom.

He, drunk with methane,
raising a man's femur like a sceptre;
she, his ravished queen,
admiring the blood-stained black roses
that could not thrive on the plains of Enna.

Assimilation

Even the Sodomites, I said, would allow
distraught refugees into their desert city,
provide them with a Sodom-made bed.

But strangers too tall, it must be admitted,
had their legs chopped off; and nationalistic Sods
stretched the heads and feet of those too small
till beds and bodies beautifully fitted.

Souls

'After the last breath, eyelids must be closed
quickly. For eyes are windows of the soul
– that shy thing which is immortal. And none
should see its exit vulnerably exposed,'

proclaimed the bearded man on Yom Kippur.
Grown-ups believed in the soul. Otherwise
why did grandfather murmur the morning prayer,
'Lord, the soul Thou hast given me is pure'?

Near the kitchen door where they notched my height
a mirror hung. There I saw the big eyes
of a boy. I could not picture the soul
immaterial and immortal. A cone of light?

Those two black zeros the soul's windows? Daft!
Later, at medical school, I learnt of
the pineal gland, its size a cherry-stone,
vestige of the third eye, and laughed.

But seven colours hide in light's disguise
and the blue sky's black. No wonder Egyptians
once believed, in their metamorphosis,
souls soared, became visible: butterflies.

Now old, I'm credulous. Superstition clings.
After the melting eyes and devastation
of Hiroshima, they say butterflies, crazed,
flew about, fluttering soundless things.

My Neighbour, Itzig

My neighbour, Itzig,
has gone queer with religion.
Yesterday he asked me
who named the angels!

Today his dog is barking and barking.

But like music that's ceased
in an adjoining room
Itzig is not here.
He is nowhere else, either.

Itzig, listen, your dog needs a walk.

But Itzig is droning on and on
– open the window, someone –
a prayer archaic and musty
and full of O.

His sad feet are on this earth,
his happy head is elsewhere
among the configuration
of the 7 palaces of light.

Come back, Itzig, your dog needs feeding.

But Itzig quests for the 8th colour.
His soul is cartwheeling, he's far
from the barely manageable
drama of the Present Tense.

Come back, Itzig, your dog needs water.

But Itzig follows, with eyes closed,
the footsteps of the sages
Amora and Rehumai
who never existed.

A Letter from Ogmore-by-Sea

Goodbye, 20th Century.
What should I mourn?
Hiroshima? Auschwitz?
Our friend, Carmi, said,
'Thank forgetfulness
else we could not live;
thank memory
else we'd have no life.'

Goodbye, 20th Century.
What shall I celebrate?
Darling, I'm out of date:
even my nostalgia
is becoming history.
Those garish, come-on posters
outside a cinema,
announce the Famous
I've never heard of.
So many other friends, too,
now like Carmi, have joined
a genealogy of ghosts.

But here, this mellow evening,
on these high cliffs I look down
to read the unrolling
holy scrolls of the sea. They are
blank. The enigma is alive
and, for the Present, I boast,
thumbs in lapels, I survive.

Delightful Eros
still hauls Reason along
zig-zag on a taut leash.
I'm still unsettled by
the silence in framed pictures,
foreground and background;
or the mastery of music
over mind. And I hail
the world within a word.
I do not need to be
a fabulist like Iolo
who, from this same coast,
would see seven sails
where there was but one.

Goodbye, 20th Century,
your trumpets and your drums,
your war-wounds still unhealed.
Goodbye, I-must-leave-you-Dolly,
goodbye Lily Marlene.
Has the Past always a future?
Will there always be
a jackboot on the stair,
a refugee to roam?
A man with no roots is lost
like the darkness in the forest
and it costs 100 years
for a hiding place
to become a home.

Now secular strangers come
sealed in Fords and Nissans,
a congregation of cars,
to this opening estuary
so various, so beautiful, so old.
The tide *is* out.
And from the sleeping reeled-
in sea – not from
the human mind's vexed fathoms –
the eternal, murderous,
fanged Tusker Rock is revealed.

An Interrupted Letter

In this room's winterlight the travail of
a letter to a new widow. Solemn,
the increasing enterprise of age.
I stutter. Consoling words come slow,
seem false, as if spoken on a stage.
It would be easier to send flowers.

I think of her closing her husband's eyelids
and I look up. Siberian snow hesitated,
then parachuted into our garden
for hours, confiscating yesterday's
footprints. Shall I send flowers?

But now my wife, unaware in the far kitchen,
suddenly sings, captivating me,
my pen mid-air above a muffled page.

When we were young, tremulant with Spring,
often off-key she'd sing her repertoire –
dateless folk songs, dance tunes dated.
In her Pears-suds bath I'd hear her,
in the Morris Minor with our kids.

I must return to my hiemal letter.
Sing on love, as once you did, sing and sing
for past youth, for hungers unabated.

Useful Knowledge

Shy Colin, the most silent of men
despite his ammunition of facts.
He'd bomb them out at dinner parties
before signing off from conversation.

'The mastrich tree, as you probably know,
is brown, resinous, and most fragrant.'
'Volapuk? Nobody speaks it now.
Lost its one thousand, five hundred words.'

At Anne's, he said, 'Tortoises often die
from diphtheria.' At our place, he told us
'Lake Titicaca's half the size of Wales –
half's in Bolivia, half in Peru.'

Last April, when his two-year-old son
lay big-eyed in the Royal Infirmary,
Colin heard the consultant whisper
to his Registrar, 'Nieman-Pick Disease.'

Colin closed his eyes, cried out shrilly,
'A genetically determined disorder
where splenectomy is palliative.
Death occurs quite early during childhood.'

Child Drawing in a Hospital Bed

Any child can open wide
the occult doors of a colour
naively to call, 'Who's there?'
For this sick girl drawing
outstep invisible ones
imprisoned everywhere.
Wasp on a windowpane.

Darkest tulip her head bends,
face white as leukaemia,
till the prince in his tower,
on parole from a story,
descends by royal crayon
and, thrilled, stays half an hour.
Wasp on a windowpane.

Birds of Rhiannon, pencilled,
alight to wake the dead –
they do not sing, she rubs them out,
they smudge into vanishings,
they swoop to Nowhere
as if disturbed by a shout.
Wasp on a windowpane.

Omens. Wild astrologies whirl:
sun and moon begin to soar.
Unlikely that maroon sky
green Christmas trees fly through
– doctors know what logic's for.
Tell me, what is magic for?
Wasp on a windowpane.

Now penal-black she profiles
four eerie malformed horses,
nostrils tethered to the ground.
Unperturbed, the child attends
for one to uplift its neck
and turn its death's head round.
Wasp on a windowpane.

Thomas Girtin's 'The White House'

Something odd about the house – so luminous
as if a truant god were resting there.

And those daffodil-bordered clouds seem intent
to spill but will, of course, never. Their oblique
presentiments of rain, their pollutions of smoke
behind, above, a huge icon of a windmill.

Though such painted scenes reject the future,
and quarrel with the ghost of Heraclitus,
now, sleep-walking into Girtin's numinous
mastery of a moment, I want narrative.

I want to forecast what the weather will bring
but all the clocks within that spotlit house,
the effulgent white house on the promontory,
have stopped at the mood of eternal evening.

The contrary sky cannot play its mobiles;
no chill wind can turn around the cross
of this indisposed windmill or stir the still
waters, the fishing boats, their capsized doubles.

I want to smell something more than paint. Loud Life!
its shyest flowers that must be held so close
before their scent is known. Life's armpits, too!
I'm troubled by the silence of this river view.

I want to trick the picture fast-forward,
shake it like a watch to make Time's nothings tick;
let the yawning god quit the house perplexed;
the complacent winds to be vexed again;

anaesthetised fishermen to go home unsurprised
to empty firegrates or expectant wives.

The Stonebreaker

Dear Inchbold,
              I want you to know about this.

23 miles from London I was walking
with Black Spot when I lingered to gaze at
a steep scarp of the chalky Downs.
I gazed and gazed until I seemed to stand
              just outside Eden.

Faraway, the beech trees in their summer
magnificence while, nearby, there happened to be
a pile of stones and a barely living tree.
It sprang out of a dead one.

              Oh Inchbold,
do you believe in the Resurrection?

Remember mild Tom, the model who died,
the one who resembled my young brother?
Suddenly, from nowhere, he appeared
and, with a noiseless hammer, struck the stones.
He did not look pathetic like the Stonebreaker
portrayed by Henry Wallis but wore fake,
unsoiled, peasant's clothes.

      Before I could speak
a bullfinch alighted on a high branch
of the strange, frail tree and Tom vanished.

You doubt what I saw? I doubt what I saw.
So much is mirage and shadow. The law
of gravity asserts itself in my mind.
I know the far hills are not really blue,
that sunlight does not truly paint the grass
an indistinct yellow. Love, itself, errs.
A child's swift daubs on paper are not Art
though the mother may think so.

      Oh Inchbold,
did I see what I saw? Tom breaking stones?

  I beg you, tell no-one of this. You know
how some believe we artists are crazy!
Besides, I may paint this experience though
Ruskin says mine is mirror's work not man's.
Write me soon. Your loving friend,
                John Brett

In the Welsh National Museum

(To Josef Herman)

Josef, in your thaumaturgic studio,
long live cobalt blue and brown!
Autumn is your season,
twilight is your hour.

Now, in my hometown, you, spooky,
conjure up, abracadabra,
this melancholy impostor
who steals my name.

Is he listening to someone
beyond the picture's frame,
playing a Chopin piano
of autumnal unhappiness?

Josef, this other is not me.
This golem hardly looks like me.
Is this your unbegotten brother
lost in menstrual blood?

If so, his passport (forged)
would have been Polish,
his exile inevitable,
his wound indescribable.

Look! My best brown coat
not yet patched at the elbow,
my cobalt blue shirt
not yet frayed at the collar.

As if challenged he, dire,
(Passport? Colour of wound?)
stares back – that look of loss –
at whomsoever stares at him.

Or across at Augustus John's
too respectable W. H. Davies,
at prettified Dylan Thomas
whose lips pout for a kiss.

Infelicitous! Wrong! Impostors
spellbound, enslaved in their world,
with no *emeth* on their foreheads,
without speech, without pneuma.

But the Welsh say, 'Whoever stares long
at his portrait will, with dismay, see
the devil.' So who's wearing my clothes?
Josef, I know your magic. I'll not stay.

Deaf Men Singing

(To Gillian)

Most poems, like golems, turn to dust at dawn
but you hallow the coarse endeavour, attend
the awkward, the not winging, the also-rans;
cheer Z because it's last; salute deaf men singing
who feel a piano's wood to hear its song,
myopic painters, their details clearly wrong,
their vast perspectives to a No–Man's Past.

Inhuman angels may command perfection
but the hollow circle drawn by Giotto
would have been more genial if hand had wavered.
So you commend sweet error, would not mend
the nervous junction, nor convert the letter O
to Death's infrangible and favoured number,
with its unseen beginning, no evident end.

Domestic

To His Wife

You need not be cross, why are you
cross–examining me?

By Ishara, queen of the oaths,
hear me out
– let's contend no more, love.

By Ishtar of Nineveh,
by Ishtar of Hattarina,

– do not shout,
what so wild as words are? –

by the hypertensive lord of Wars,
by St Elmo and by Santa Claus,

after the doors of dawn re-opened
– let's cease our battling, love –

I was still bloody-well rattling
bars of a stationary lift
between electrically-lit, empty floors.

To His Friend's Wife

No letters, no photos, no keepsake.

No whistling of a coded tune,
no signals of lover to his lass.

I think you're glad I didn't
when the sea surrendered to the moon.

No scratches, no love-bites, no heartache.

I think I'm glad I didn't
when the church clock tolled the hour.

Your ring shone muffled gold not wanton brass.

Judgement Night we'll not shuffle
to the bench, bent, crass, trembling,
beg pardon, your honour.

We'll stand there upright, alas.

New Granddaughter

You don't know the score, what's you, what's not.
Remote ancestors return you can't disown.
This prelude, this waiting for an encore.

Is that raised hand yours, this wind-pecked morning?
Enigmatic trees, askew, shake above the pram.
All's perplexity, green reverie, shadowland.

But why this grandfatherly spurt of love?
Your skin is silk, your eyes suggest they're blue.
I bend to smell small apricots and milk.

Did I dream that legend of the Angel
who falls to touch each baby's fontanelle
and wipe out racial memory, leaving *déjà vu*?

I'm confessing! Your newness, petite, portends
my mortality – a rattle for you, the bell for me.
Hell, I'm old enough to mutter blessings.

The determinates of the clock increase.
Sometimes you close your eyes noiselessly, turn
your head, listening to music that has ceased.

Presences

I'm halted by the unintentional
honeyed malice of mementos:
this awkward night-school painting
by my genial father-in-law;
this vast desk my mother fussed
to give me. 'Fit for an emperor!'

And here's another hook to chin:
a door opens in the next room
and I hear a snatch of Gershwin –
that tune our car-bound family used
to sing. On music's heartless beat
my keen dead come marching in.

O button-holing familiars,
your blurs I sense, your ashes I taste.
So much I owe, so much forgotten
that I owe. But now dear ghosts go
that I may live. Be brief guests.
Leave with a burglar's haste.

The future's future is another place
where other absences will sting; where
some unfocused progeny perhaps
will summon me, stumbling on
some inherited thing or, less likely,
reading this poem, maybe!

Last Lunch

In memory of David Wright

That last late lunch we had in Soho
you spoke of friends who had gone before,
edgy prisoners of poetry.

Would readers forget their astute verse-skill,
Jock Graham, Tom Blackburn, Stevie,
who taking the maverick route

from a poisoned tree made a table
and, at that table, ate its fruit?

Then you said, 'My turn, Dannie',
reaching for the bill.

Why Angels Disappeared

When first the celestial orchestra played
decorously the angels began to dance.

This was the time when the moon unmuzzled
glowed twice more luminously than now.

But wanton Azazel, the angel of Vice,
unhooked his nice masterpiece wings, displayed,

enticed daft angels to swig double-strength nectar,
deft angels to juggle the fruits of Paradise.

Hallelujah! Hallelujah! That unquiet night
(such an orgy) half the angels got laid

and their pet unicorns ran riot, began to bite,
called for pale maidens to make life rosier.

Their randy horns grew and grew. Some howled at
the moon, some crapped on the ambrosia.

Soon the Archangel's police arrived, blew
whistles for music to cease, moonlight to fade

and foolishly fed the frenetic unicorns
tinned human flesh, calming pesticides.

Later, the angels ate all the unicorns,
suffered CJD. Not one of them survived.

The Arrival and Departure of Adam and Eve at Dover

I

At the gate, expelled from the fable
of the East, the man's profile turned towards
the ullulating distraught woman.

And behind this couple now stumbling forward
– she half-bent over in her weeping –
the distant blitz-light of an angel.

II

So many thousands of centuries passed
and, in their innocence, new friends eased them
of the bdellium, the onyx stone
and the little gold acquired in Havilah.

So many more miles of thorns and thistles,
so many more winters howled away
before they came, at last, penniless,
to the altered paparazzi at Dover.

The fuss! The fuss! The woman moaned on,
inconsolable, but the man seemed composed
until secular officials decreed
they faced no danger in their native country.

The Home Secretary (appealed to) said,
'At the end of the day' and 'God is merciful'.
Ceremonious duty done the two
'economic migrants' were repatriated.

On TV newsreels see them stepping from
a police van, discharged from this little world,
this sceptre'd isle, this other Eden,
still in disgrace, coats over their heads.

Soho: Saturday Night

Always Cain, anonymous amidst the poor,
Abel dead in his eye, and over his damned sore
a khaki muffler, loiters, a fugitive in Soho,
enters The Golden Calf Club and hears Esau,

dishevelled and drunk, cursing kith and kin.
'A mess of pottage!' Esau strokes an unshaven chin
and strikes a marble table-top. Then hairy hands
fidget dolefully, raise up a glass of gin.

Outside, Joseph, dyspnoeic, regards a star
convexing over Dean Street, coughs up a flower
from ruined lungs – rosy petals on his tongue –
recalls the Pit and wounds of many a colour.

Traffic lights change. With tapping white stick
a giant crosses the road between the frantic
taxis. A philistine pimp laughs. Dancing
in The Nude Show Delilah suddenly feels sick.

Ruth, too, the innocent, was gullibly led,
lay down half-clothed on a brassy railing bed
of Mr Boaz of Bayswater. Now, too late, weeps
antiseptic tears, wishes she were dead.

Who goes home? Nebuchadnezzar to the doss-
house where, all night, he'll turn and toss.
Lunchtime, in Soho Square, he munched the grass
and now he howls at strangers as they pass.

In Café Babylon, Daniel, interpreter of dreams,
listens to Belshazzar, a shy lad in his teens:
'A soiled finger moved across the lavatory wall.'
Growing up is not so easy as it seems.

Prophets, like tipsters, awaiting the Advent.
Beggar Job, under the flashing advertisement
for toothpaste, the spirochaete in his brain,
groans. Chalks a lurid picture on the pavement.

The Golden Calf closes. Who goes home? All
tourists to Nod; psalmists from their pub crawl;
they leave unshaved Soho to its dawn furnace
of affliction, its wormwood and its gall.

1948, 1995

Inscription on the Flyleaf of a Bible

(For Larne)

Doubting, read what this fabled history teaches,
how the firework, Imagination, reaches high
to dignify and sanctify.

You need not, granddaughter, be religious
to learn what Judges, Kings, Prophets, yield,
thought-lanterns for Life's darker field,
moral lies of piety and poetry.

You need not, granddaughter, hosanna heroes:
this wily shepherd, that bloodthirsty tough;
yet applaud the bulrush child
who, when offered gold, chose the coal.
Satisfied, the tyrant Pharaoh smiled,
did not see the pattern in the whole.

Forgive the triumphalism and the pride,
forgo the curses and the ritual stuff.
You, older, I hope, will always side
with the enslaved and hunted,
deride the loud and lethal crowd
who vilify and simplify.

What is poetry but the first words
Adam, amazed, spoke to Eve?
On the first page of Genesis
hear the next to Nothing.
Later sound-effects, God off-stage, or theurgic stunts,
(water from a rock, a bush ablaze) might deceive
but bring ladders only to nerveless heaven.
Better to walk with Jephthah's luckless daughter
among real hills. And grieve.

Enjoy David's winging gifts to praise;
Solomon's rapturous serenade; also Job's
night-starred elegance of distress —
though such eloquence can bless,
indiscriminately, the last flags of the just
and the unjust on the barricade.

Read, granddaughter, these scandalous stories,
screaming Joseph in the pit of scorpions,
champion Goliath of course outclassed;
so many cubits of sorrow and delight,
so many visions of our ruffian Past.
They do not stale or fade
and may fortify and mollify.

Events Leading to the Conception of Solomon, the Wise Child

And David comforted Bathsheba his wife, and went into
her, and lay with her; and she bore a son, and he called
his name Solomon: and the Lord loved him

I

Are the omina favourable?
Scribes know the King's spittle,
even the most honoured
like Seraiah the Canaanite,
and there are those, addicted,
who inhale
          the smoke of burning papyrus.

So is the date-wine sour, the lemon sweet?
Who can hear the sun's furnace?

The shadow of some great bird
          drifts indolently
across the ochres and umbers
of the afternoon hills
          that surround Jerusalem.
Their rising contours, their heat-refracting
          undulations.

The lizard is on the ledges,
the snake is in the crevices.

It is where Time lives.

Below, within the thermals of the Royal
        City,
past the cursing camel driver,
past the sweating woman carrying water
        in a goatskin,
past the leper peeping through
        the lateral slats
of his fly-mongering latrine
to the walls of the Palace itself,
the chanting King is at prayer.

        Aha, aha,
attend to my cry, O Lord
who makest beauty
to be consumed away like a moth;
purge me with hyssop and I
        shall be clean.
Wash me and I shall be whiter
        than the blossom.
Blot out my iniquities.

Not yet this prayer, not yet
        that psalm.
It is where a story begins.
Even the bedouin beside their black tents
have heard the desert wind's rumour.
They ask:
        Can papyrus grow
where there is no marsh?
They cry:
        Sopher yodea
to the Scribe with two tongues,
urge him to tend his kingdom
of impertinence.

II

When the naked lady stooped to bathe
    in the gushings of a spring,
the voyeur on the tower roof
    just happened to be the King.

She was summoned to the Palace
    where the King displayed his charms;
he stroked the harp's glissandos,
    sang her a couple of psalms.

Majestic sweet-talk in the Palace
    – he name-dropped Goliath and Saul –
till only one candle-flame flickered
    and two shadows moved close on the wall.

Of course she hankered for the Palace.
    Royal charisma switched her on.
Her husband snored at the Eastern Front,
    so first a kiss, then scruples gone.

Some say, 'Sweet victim in the Palace,'
    some say, 'Poor lady in his bed.'
But Bathsheba's teeth like milk were white,
    and her mouth like wine was red.

David, at breakfast, bit an apple.
    She, playful, giggling, seized his crown,
then the apple-flesh as usual
    after the bite turned brown.

III

In the kitchen, the gregarious, hovering flies
where the servants breakfast.
A peacock struts
            in its irradiance,
and is ignored.

On the stone floor and on the shelves
the lovely shapes of utensils,
great clay pots, many jugs of wine
            many horns of oil,
the food-vessels and the feast-boards.

On the long table, butter of kine, thin loaves,
bowls of olives and griddle-cakes,
wattled baskets of summer fruit,
flasks of asses' milk and jars of honey.

What a tumult of tongues,
        the maids and the men,
the hewers of wood,
the drawers of water,
        the narrow-skulled
        and the wide-faced.
What a momentary freedom prospers,
        a detour from routine,
a substitute for mild insurrection.

They ask:
    In his arras-hung chamber
    did the King smell of the sheepcote?
    On the ivory bench, did he seat her
        on cushions?
    Did she lie on the braided crimson couch,
    beneath her head pillows of goat hair?

Who saw him undo her raiments?
Who overheard Uriah's wife,
Bathsheba of the small voice,
         cry out?
Was it a woman made love to
or the nocturnal moan
         of the turtle dove?
Will the priest, Nathan, awaken
who, even in his sleep, mutters
         Abomination?

Now she who is beautiful to look upon
leaves furtively by a back door.
She will become a public secret.
She wears fresh garments of blue and purple,
the topaz of Ethiopia beneath her apparel.
But a wind gossips in the palm trees,
the anaphora of the wind
         in the fir-trees of Senir,
         in the cedars of Lebanon,
         in the oaks of Bashan.
It flaps the tents where Uriah, the Hittite,
is encamped with Joab's army
on the Eastern open fields.

Does purity of lust last one night only?
In the breakfasting kitchen, the peacock screams.

IV

The wind blows and the page turns over.
  Soon the King was reading a note.
Oh such excruciating Hebrew:
  'I've one in the bin,' she wrote.

Since scandal's bad for royal business
  the King must not father the child;
so he called Uriah from the front,
  shook his hand like a voter. Smiled.

Uriah had scorned the wind's whisper,
  raised his eyebrows in disbelief.
Still, here was the King praising his valour,
  here was the King granting him leave.

In uniform rough as a cat's tongue
  the soldier artlessly said,
'Hard are the stones on the Eastern Front,
  but, Sire, harder at home is my bed.'

Though flagons and goat-meat were offered
  the Hittite refused to go home.
He lingered outside the Palace gates,
  big eyes as dark as the tomb.

Silk merchants came and departed,
  they turned from Uriah appalled –
for the soldier sobbed in the stony heat,
  ignored his wife when she called;

sat down with his sacks, sat in the sun,
    sat under stars and would not quit,
scowled at the King accusingly
    till the King got fed up with it.

'Stubborn Uriah, what do you want?
    Land? Gold? Speak and I'll comply.'
Then two vultures creaked overhead
    to brighten the Hittite's eye.

'Death.' That's what he sought in the desert
    near some nameless stony track.
And there two vultures ate the soldier
    with a dagger in his back.

The widow was brought to the Palace,
    a Queen for the King-size bed,
and oh their teeth like milk were white,
    and their mouths like wine were red.

V

Should there be merriment at a funeral?
Stones of Jerusalem, where is your lament?
Should her face not have been leper-ashen?
Should she not have torn at her apparel
        bayed at the moon?
Is first young love
        always a malady?

When Uriah roared with the Captains of Joab,
        the swearing garrisons,
the dust leaping behind the chariots,
        the wagons, the wheels;
when his sword was unsheathed
amidst the uplifted trumpets
and the cacophony of donkeys;
when he was fierce as a close-up,
        huge with shield and helmet;
when his face was smeared with vermilion,
did she think of him less
        than a scarecrow in a field?

When she was more girl than woman
who built for her
        a house of four pillars?
When his foot was sore
        did she not dip it in oil?
When his fever seemed perilous
        did she not boil the figs?

When the morning stars sang together,
face to face, they sang together.
At night when she shyly stooped
        did he not boldly soar?

When, at midnight, the owl screeched
        who comforted her?
When the unclothed satyr danced
        in moonlight
who raised a handkerchief to her wide eyes?

When the archers practised
      in the green pastures
whose steady arm curled about her waist?

True love is not briefly displayed
like the noon glory of the fig marigold.

Return oh return
pigeons of memory to your homing land.

But the scent was only a guest
      in the orange tree.
The colours faded
      from the ardent flowers
not wishing to outstay their visit.

VI

The wind blows and the page turns over.
   To Bathsheba a babe was born.
Alas, the child would not feed by day,
   by night coughed like a thunderstorm.

'Let there be justice after sunset,'
   cried Nathan, the raging priest.
Once again he cursed the ailing child
   and the women's sobs increased.

So the skeletal baby sickened
   while the King by the cot-side prayed
and the insomniac mother stared
   at a crack in the wall afraid.

Nobody played the psaltery,
  nobody dared the gameboard.
The red heifer and doves were slaughtered.
  A bored soldier cleaned his stained sword.

Courtiers huddled in the courtyard,
  rampant their whisperings of malice.
The concubines strutted their blacks.
  The spider was in the Palace.

Soon a battery of doors in the Palace,
  soon a weird shout, 'The child is dead.'
Then Bathsheba's teeth like milk were white,
  and her eyes like wine were red.

Outside the theatre of the shrine
  David's penitent spirit soared
beyond the trapped stars. He wept. He danced
  the dance of death before the Lord.

That night the King climbed to her bedroom.
  Gently he coaxed the bereaved
and in their shared and naked suffering
  the wise child, love, was conceived.

CODA

Over the rocky dorsals of the hills
the pilgrim buses of April arrive,
one by one, into Jerusalem.

There was a jackal on the site
          of the Temple
before the Temple was built.

And stones. The stones only.

Are the omina favourable?
Will there be blood on the thorn bush?
Does smoke rising from the rubbish dump
          veer to the West or to the East?
So much daylight! So much dust!
This scribe is
          and is not
the Scribe who knew the King's spittle.

After the soldier alighted,
a black-bearded, invalid-faced man,
stern as Nathan, head covered,
followed by a fat woman, a tourist
wearing the same Phoenician purple
          as once Bathsheba did,
her jewelled wrist, for one moment,
a drizzle of electric.

But no bizarre crowned phantom
will sign the Register
          at the King David Hotel.

Like the lethargic darkness
of 3000 years ago,
once captive, cornered
within the narrow-windowed
        Temple of Solomon,
everything has vanished into the light.

Except the stones. The stones only.

There is a bazaar-loud haggling
        in the chiaroscuro
        of the alleyways,
tongue-gossip in the gravel walks,
even in the oven of the Squares,
a discontinuous, secret weeping
of a husband or wife, belittled and betrayed
behind the shut door of an unrecorded house.

There is a kissing of the stones,
a kneeling on the stones,
        psalmody and hymnody,
winged prayers swarming in the domed hives
of mosques, synagogues, churches,
ebullitions of harsh religion.

– For thou art my lamp, O Lord . . .
– In the name of God, Lord of the Worlds . . .
– Hear the voice of my supplications . . .
– And forgive us our trespasses . . .
– The Lord is my shepherd I shall not want . . .
– My fortress, my high tower, my deliverer . . .
– The Lord is my shepherd I shall not . . .
. . . my buckler, my hiding place . . .
– I am poured out like water . . .
– The Lord is my shepherd . . .
. . . and my bones are vexed . . .
– The Lord is . . .
      – Allah Akbar!
      – Sovereign of the Universe!
      – Our Father in Heaven!
      – Father of Mercies!
      – Shema Yisroael!

There is a tremendous hush in the hills
      above the hills
where the lizard is on the ledges,
where the snake is in the crevices,
after the shadow of an aeroplane
      has hurtled and leapt
below the hills and on to the hills
      that surround Jerusalem.

Part Two

New Poems

1998 – 2002

Just a Moment

As my wife arranges the lilac in a vase
I think how for years I've stared from this window
at that garden tree so stark it seemed ashamed;
or as now in May, proud – dressed to the nines,
rustling its green silks and in stately bloom.

I've stood here observing Time's sorcery,
the petroleum sunset behind its branches,
the midges energetic above the grass,
or the rising moon a phoenix in its high leaves.

I have grown old watching such things
and thought how a poet's late adagios
like those of Beethoven (*Muss es sein?*)
should say more about the seasons of fate
than the years have wings and the hours pass.

But now I'm attentive to the window itself
and, for a moment, I've cracked it again, trespassed
into the half-mad timeless world that is still
where I am not old nor will be older –
the tip of my tongue against the glass,
the chill touch of it, the nothing taste of it,
until I breathe in the jubilant Yes
and mortally precarious fragrance of lilac
my wife has just placed upon the windowsill.

A Figure of 8

In Mr Theophilus's jail
of the sun-striped classroom
the boy half listens to a story
of royalty-loving Christopher Robin.
Then, after musical scales
(his friend, Fatty Jones, is scolded –
Fatty Jones is sobbing),
sings, 'Let the prairie echo,
God bless the Prince of Wales!'

Free, at last, arms horizontal,
he jet-roars out of school
into a vigorous sunset,
soars between the Hs
of the Millennium Stadium,
loops the loop, flies to Africa
to see naked women
(whom gently he caresses);
turns left at Albany Road,
farts H_2Ss.

The evening's shot down in flames
butcher's reds in the clouds are dark,
smoke is rising from the drains,
someone has bombed the park.

Both the swings are on fire,
the empty see-saw is charred;
the enemy is a brute,
the enemy must be foiled;
blood is streaming down the chute,
the wooden horses are running wild.

There's a furnace in the churchyard
(a sorcerer has cast his spell)
the mandrake's screaming and the yew,
the graves are sinking down to hell.

Unseen, a spaceship from another world
flees the heights, drags a spooky trace.
Below the pond is poisoned and the dew.
Safely the boy comes home to base.

There beneath the night's first star,
observed by his patient cat,
he chalks across the garden shed
FUCK WINNIE THE POOH.
Then adds for luck and Fatty Jones
FUCK MR THEOPHILUS TOO.

Blond Boys

In Stockholm
I saw my first shy love hobble by
hand in hand with her small blond grandson.

Eva Jones, remember me?
My acne. Your dimples.

When your rode your important Raleigh bike
to school, your skirt high,
I held my breath.

With heroic intensity of a 15 year old,
dared by you, I climbed the glass-crowned wall
and stole Mrs Humphreys' summer apples.

Oh the forever of an August Sunday evening
when near the back door's delinquent scent
of honeysuckle, forehead to forehead
I searched your searching eyes.

All the next week similitudes of love,
the jailer of reason,

until plain as the prose of a synopsis,
you bluntly said (with impressive sighs)
'You have a beautiful classy mind
but I find you physically unattractive –
and I prefer, um, blond boys besides.'

Among a Heap of Stones

'I've lost my soul,' the sick man said
(the soul does not like a sick body),
'but somewhere in the world, some winter place,
surely there must be a potion, or a herb,
or a mineral, which can cure me?'

Alert, we came to a tame cold wilderness
(in every city there is so much rubble)
and I, a doctor, picked up a nameless stone,
weighed it in my hand, felt it, smelt it,

then chose another, one almost the same,
but darker, odourless, and touched by frost
– as if there was (speak to me of music)
such a thing as a stone mysterious
among a heap of stones which, if found,
would let a man reclaim what he has lost.

Prayer in the Waiting Room

Banished from health I enter the unknown
as the two did stumbling from Paradise.
Never in my life have I felt so alone.

In this doctor's waiting room, many-eyed,
my censored secrets are married to my fears
like a shotgun bridegroom to his bride.

When I was a child I thought blue, I said green
and with magician's sleight of hand, jubilant,
would squeeze apple-pips from a tangerine!

Now, doctor, magic me. Let me be released
from clawing ills, let home again be Eden-like
where, thankfully, I may fast for God or feast.

Terrible Angels

One bedtime, my father showed me his war medals,
their pretty coloured ribbons, and told me
the other story about the angels of Mons,
that élite and puissant expedition from God:
how first their invisible presence caused horses
to bolt and flocks of meat-snatching birds to rise,
circle around and around like a carousel.

But war coarsens (he said) even genteel angels.
When they spoke it was the silence of gas, amen;
when they sang it was shrapnel striking helmets;
then, finally, soldiers' prayers and soldiers' screams
thrilled the cold angels to steal the muskets
of the dead, to become stealthily visible,
bold and bloodthirsty, true facsimiles of men.

(My father, invalided home, was told
he knew more about angels than was healthy.)

The Relic

*(A variation of Ewald Osers' translation of
'Paradise Lost' by J. Seifert)*

I, Jaroslav Seifert,
opened the pages of the bible
and my mother, my expert,
taught me the cognominal codes
of the Old Testament women.

Adah signifies rich ornament;
Ophrah, gentle mare of the red deer;
Abigail, true source of joy
(Come out to play, come out to play);
and Naamah, one whose beauty
could lead the open-mouthed angels astray.

But when, years later, blow after blow,
they dragged away the Jews,
their children scared and helpless,
not one of us dared
to call out a modest 'No'.

Tamar signifies palm tree
with its dates, its sugar and wine;
Zilpah, a little droplet
of such a little drop;
Jemima means peaceful dove, pure and divine;
and Tirzah, pleasure-giving (as in love).

But they dragged away the Jews.

Tallest behind the barbed wire
Jecholiah, half-skeleton, his big eyes
so soon to feed the flies. Such a joke!
His name signifies 'The Lord is All-Powerful'.

Rachel means warm woolly ewe-lamb;
Delilah, ringlets, falling tresses,
their darknesses and their points of light;
Deborah, a swarm of honey bees;
Esther, starbright starbright.

And I almost forgot, Shoshana.
Oh Shoshana means rose,
the only flower left to us on this earth
from the Eden that was.

One of the Chosen

He candled away my fears one by one.
Torch-fire and swastikas, that's how it began.
In capsizing dark his guiding lights blazed out.
A thousand *Sieg Heils*. Soluble all doubt.

Herr Doktor, I did not know the railway lines led
to infinity. But when the stink of the dead
tracked the wind, I wondered. I lost my appetite.
Maggot imaginings, tortured me at night.

Then the decree: *More gas vans*. The task was mine.
I queried, 'Sir?' He said, 'Yes.' How could I decline?
He jerked on wires, I had to fall or leap.
I had no tears of my own to weep.

When he raised his arm my fingerprints left
the shocking clue. When he felt bereft
I groaned a dirge; when he laughed I shook
with merriment. But six million? That's a joke.

Few resist the trapped compulsion of the crowd.
Ein Volk, ein Reich, ein Führer. I was proud:
the SS comradeship, discipline and skill.
We suffered too. Praise God, my family love me still.

You sneer. I did my duty. What I was I am,
one who knew the sequel to *Non Serviam.*
Elect I was chosen as his instrument.
Herr Doktor, an S is but a straight line bent.

The Story of Lazarus

After the war he settled in kindly Cardiff
his English uncertain, his Welsh not at all.
For three years a clerk who hardly said a word.

Then, accusingly, he showed us the number
on his arm, spoke of how he had survived
in his chemistry, the sudden sound of
his heartbeat. Each stark detail. We were shocked.

Week after week this man's monstrous story
heard in Whitchurch, Llandaf, Canton, Cathays,
in pubs and clubs – The Three Elms, The Conway,
The Golden Shark, the Post House, the Moat House;
told even to Cardiff's patient statues:
John Batchelor, Lloyd George, Nye Bevan.

We closed our eyes till we, too, became stone.

So he whispered his dark story to our children
and years later to our children's children.
Soon they merely nodded, eager to join
the procession banging its way outside
to the Firework Display above Roath Park,
the oompha, oompha, down the street fading.

My Cousin, the Soldier

When my cousin, the soldier, returned,
no showers of paper fluttered downwards,
no flags were strung across the street.

At his house no energetic Dalmatian
came bounding out, wagging its tail.
But they say a stranger stepped in front of him
on the front path, took out a key,
and opened the front door. Closed it.

They say my cousin, the soldier, stood still,
observed the front room's surprising curtains;
looked to the right – the neighbour was cutting a hedge,
looked to the left – the traffic lights changed.

I've never believed such stories.
I still don't believe in them.
I remember my cousin, the soldier.
When he was a child he would sleep
with his eyes and mouth wide open like a dead fish.

Torch

They told how her grandfather's town
had been put to the torch. 'Put to the torch?'
Unsmiling refugees in long overcoats
fleeing with their junky cartloads,
limping down the cratered roads ceaselessly.

But she was as young as an Australian.
My autumn was her springtime.
She knew the valour of her cherry tree in blossom.
I knew my sumac tree would soon turn red.

'When I was a child,' she said,
'sometimes under the bedclothes
I would shine a torch on my fingers
to see the blood in them.'

Ants

*What would be left of our tragedies if a literate insect were to
present us his?*   Cioran

My gentle wife, convinced pacifist, finds
all ants loathsome. When on crawling duty
for their Queen they remind her of armies
carrying home their carrion booty.

So, imperturbably, my wife, anti-ant,
stamps on them mercilessly. Some become blurs;
but she can't annihilate all those moving
columns of black-uniformed scavengers.

Down and down her thudding foot bombs
the wingless neuters. They must shed calories
as, desperate, they flee and excavate
safe Maginot trenches, darkest galleries.

Now my wife (sweet to kiss) pours boiling water
over them. Most die noiselessly for their Queen
as my darling floods the kitchen floor, napalms
the step to Dis outside the door with steam.

Still surviving ants panic and scurry
but will soon regroup as if commanded, return
like hoodwinked soldiers to the battlefield
for the Queen's employment. They'll bleed and burn.

War Poet

Bring your TV cameras, bring your microphones.
Soldiers to the broad gate, soldiers to the fire.
Oblivion is their name, vultures to their bones,
while far behind, with proper melancholy,
the ineffectual poet strums his lyre.

Three Full Moon Haikus

Low moon over sea.
Tall masts swing in the harbour
and play ball with it.

In this closed seaside Town,
in the listening, 4 a.m., leper-empty,
interior streets that copy
each other; on inverted Vs
of rooftops – the static moonlight.

In residence also, the emphatic moon
at the Town's silent Football Stadium.
Now, crossing the nearby railway bridge
the oblique silhouette
of the blinded hunter
four times the size of a man.

He stumbles in error
after the staring moon.
Nightwatchman, where are you
to direct him Eastward?
He cannot see
how the moon travels below,
on and on the parallel, polished
railway lines away.

Moon so magnified,
coming from afar. What a
night for goalkeepers!

Moon in close-up, stay a moment
bisected by the church spire.
Before your haunting's up, raise
the churchyard dead, immaterial,
with your lodestone.

Tarry, captive chaperone.
Let the stars tremble and go home
alone. Before the church clock
strikes and gongs five times
exert your witchery.

Ah, here comes a slow cloud
of see-through ectoplasm.
Ah, going going gone,
sighs the happy little,
busy little, pink worm.

Blue sky. But the moon
all morning, like a dunce ghost,
outstays Night's seance.

Fly

He was talking about Kierkegaard
when I observed a housefly had chosen
to settle on his elegant left shoe.

He was saying how we are a mixture
of the finite and the infinite
unaware of this fly, a masterpiece.

He was saying we are a synthesis
of the temporal and the eternal
while the fly's proboscis sucked his shoe.

And when it crawled on to his exposed sock
I thought how the female domesticus,
programmed, lays its eggs in refuse or dung;

how the larvae, those small white maggots,
change to pupae without casting their skins
till eight days later the perfect fly emerges.

Itzig Takes to Philosophy

When asked what he had learned
at the Adult Evening Class (Philosophy)
Itzig defined 'Felaptron'.

It is a mnemonic, he said,
that represents the fourth mood
in the third syllogistic figure
in which a negative general major premise
and an affirmative general minor premise
yield a negative singular conclusion –

unlike 'Ferison', a mnemonic
that represents the sixth mood
of the third syllogistic figure
in which a negative general major premise
and an affirmative singular minor premise
yield a negative singular conclusion.

Of all this, continued Itzig, I was ignorant
till I joined the Adult Evening Class (Philosophy).

Random Birthday Thoughts

Leaving the pavement to negotiate
revolving doors of the Angel Hotel
I thought of all those millions born (not cloned)
crying, 'I am' the same laboured minute,
and of those going out from this world
as others were coming in – as if, compelled,
they had pushed on God's revolving doors
so some, suffering, could quit more easily.

I thought too, of God's noxious bacteria
which I had seen earlier that morning,
all appearing to be identical
beneath an astonished microscope
like the swart pips of archaic apples,
perdurable detritus of Eden.

And then I thought of how, when I was a boy,
I'd been told to use the word 'unique' rarely
since everything is; and of Abraham
ruining his father's business, wild
with an axe in the prosperous idol shop,
screaming The Lord is One, The Lord is One.

Snapshot of Ruskin in Venice

That man now coming out of the Hotel
will soon be Art's spy, happily disguised,
a long black cloth over his head, taking
daguerrotypes. High up, he'll measure
and draw and pry, assent to the savagery
of the Gothic. Venetians, below, passing by
will gaze at this headless figure surprised.

On Sunday in church with pious Effie
he kneeled beside decaying candles.
The drone and moan of Latin resembled grief.
The chunky priest in his sable and satin
had not heard the geologists' hammers
destroying the pages of the bible.
Not for him the abyss of disbelief.
Rather the old rudimentary fable
where God consoles and the Devil rages.

And last night in the marble ballroom
a spunky clan of competing officers
frontally displayed their peacock's tail
for Effie – her eyes dancing above the fan.
Eros in handcuffs and without his wit.
Where the barrel organ and the monkey?

Flirty Austrians! Their waltzes and their polkas!
Well, let her have her fling. But party over,
chandelier-blind, stumbling into dark,
her foot so light in the ballroom clumsily
crushed a snail – the spinal noise of it!
And she who'd been so vivacious cried.

Tittle-tattle, now this feminine thing
wearisome. Limply, he tried to comfort her
who needed to be more than gently kissed.
'Please, Effie dear,' wondering helplessly
was it the silly snail that made her weep?

Soon, bonded, they boarded their gondola
but, above, a shackled gargoyle laughed.
He looked up, saw the stone leer and higher
a crazed star fall and fall from the jail
of the sky making its bid for freedom.

Prufrock at the Seaside

A beautiful woman should be looking at me
as I think big thoughts and stare at the sea.

On this cliff I feel like a movie star
but without my glasses I can't see far.

Perhaps if I had a little more hair
and owned a Rolls-Royce like a millionaire

those bikini ladies mincing by
would, like greedy bees, to my honey fly.

Once I wore the bottoms of my trousers rolled
but my legs are thin and feel the cold.

'You should have married Maisie,' said her friend,
'personified contentment, love without end.'

Pectoral young men play football on the beach
under circling seagulls crying each to each.

'Maisie sweet,' I'd said, 'marry me' but she turned sour,
looked as cheerful as Schopenhauer.

Afterwards, forever, for the sake of my health
I thought it best to mate with myself.

A small boy throws a stone to skim the sea,
a black dog runs after it uselessly.

I remember the sandwiches my mother made,
my teeth grinding sand, red bucket and spade

and in the car going home we all would sing
'Stormy Weather'. Me as Sinatra or Bing.

The football players' shadows run and grow long.
Suddenly the prom's coloured lamps come on.

Look! That scandalous couple. He's stroking her breast.
Oh King David, voyeur, I see them undressed.

The sundown's punctual, the clouds are dyed.
I'm no Don Juan – but what if I'd tried?

I still dream of Maisie, rose with a thorn,
she a queen to lead me, I her willing pawn.

The waves lash on but the sea's in its chains.
The beach becomes desolate. The dog remains.

Pushkin to his Promiscuous Aglaya

My Aglaya, you could not resist this one
– his uniform, his black curly moustache;
or that one – so attractively stashed with cash.
And he who needs only whisper in French to score.
Also Cleon – such conversational skill;
and Damis whose throaty singing could thrill
you to pieces. But tell me, my dear,
What did your husband wed *you* for?

I know how you were always bowled over
by sportsmen and swordsmen. So you were had,
my dear, by that kilted somersaulting peer
(easy to adore) and by those Englishmen
you called Sir Lancelot and Galahad
(though both, I think, a little queer).
Well, there are 365 knights in a year.
What did you wed your husband for?

Flowers

For my wife white freesias.
Mid-day, in a vase, their shadows flew
   to the serenity of a blank wall
when the fitful sun barged in, came through.

To my doubting father,
the hymns of bluebells, companionable.
   What greater silences than these?
Nothing better could be his tutor.

To my pious mother,
blithe daffodils from beneath the trees,
   emblems of sighing Spring. What else
could I do? Bitter, she was dying.

For my elder daughter,
a fortune-telling chain of daisies.
   Demure flirts, unbuttoned and bold,
so fresh with the dew of the garden.

For my younger daughter,
a buttercup with its golden ray
   turned on, to hold beneath the chin.
What good husband will give her butter?

For my little son enthralled,
Time's zany token of renascence
   and decay – a dandelion clock
to puff at, puff at, and blow it all away.

The Yellow Bird

I do not want it
the witchcraft song of the yellow bird,
nor this room of whisperings
as the slanting rain punctual
pelts against the windowpane.

I do not want it
the heavy brocaded curtains motionless,
her face in profile, Egyptian-like,
unsmiling, emotionless,
staring into the sorry street.

I do not want it
these mirrors without reflections,
these clothes ritually torn, rage in rags,
this piano-lid closed,
a coffin of music.

They say the yellow bird in anger
can only sing sweetly. Not so.

It sang piercingly
in the garden, at the cool of the day,
when Adam, fearful, hid among the bushes.

It sang raucously,
turning its dreadful, juridic beak
in the ululating caves of the troglodytes.

And it sang eerily
in the courts of Osiris, the sunsetter,
the lord of the dead, the judge of souls.

There are no frontiers, my friend, for the yellow bird.

It sang, hovering above the fire,
its wings beating just above the fire,
before the warriors ate their prisoners.

Later, it sang the glory of the celestial
for St Paul in his trance
to become his pet bird, his ally and harbinger.

It sings still at the River Styx
as the ferry crosses and the dog barks;
and in the evening ghost-mists
of long ago deserted battlefields.

It sings in every hospital at 3 a.m.
the song of incurable darkness.

I do not want it
the four coal-black limousines
now hushing their way
to a crematorium.

I do not want it
the overt horror in the beauty
of the wreath.

I do not want it, I do not want it,
the congregation that dare not weep,
the weariness of the God-man,
his mechanical laudation,
his secret ennui of disbelief.

Sing noiselessly, yellow bird,
if sing you must. Or sleep.

1945, 2001

The Appointment

Since the last place I want to be
is where I'm heading towards
why do I welcome the road signs
which point to that destination?

And since the best I can hope for
is to arrive late, if not later,
why am I pressing down my foot
on the damned accelerator?

Enemies

Remembering dirty deeds and verbal blows
Heine said he'd be glad to forgive his enemies
once their bodies were swinging on a gallows.

I have an affinity with Heine.
To forgive my enemies is my quest.

But no need for them to swing on gallows
pecked to meat by magpies and by crows.
A Garden of Rest will do – one well-cared
for, well-aired – fragrance of cut grass,
gravel pathways, elaborate headstones.

No expense spared. I'll pay.
(Such charity they say is blessed.)
I'm so longing to be virtuous.
I'm so impatient to pardon them.

Phone Call

At 3 a.m., the hour of the rising Dead,
Hello, Hello? No-one spoke.

Beyond the limits of the ordinary
a stranger would have stood, skull to toe,
transfixed in the doorway
like a lit enlarged Xray film!

Hello? Hello? I wait and know
the intimidation of silence.

                Discharged
from the lunatic asylum of sleep
now alert, adrenal, I explore
the moonstruck window.

Outside, the sighing, fussy
surge of the sea swarming up
the unpeopled, pebbled shore.

Certain nights the house creaks
and the nearer I move to the dead hour
the smaller I become.

I've eaten my prunes, Daddy.
I've taken my cod-liver oil.

The clock's disarmed.
The night-bird is flying to the moon

and wind and cloud play lighting tricks
above the inebriated-dancing sea
that flaunts mock silver on its blacks.

Infidelity

That night away Beth thought of her children
and how her husband, John, would put them to bed.

Then through the restaurant window saw the wind
shake down wedding blossom from a cherry tree.

And Tom, through the window saw a telephone booth
and thought of the lies he'd invent for his wife.

And Beth spoke of the alarm signals of hidden birds
when the next door cat prowled in her garden.

And Tom thought of his garden, its tall ash tree
and how its bossy roots endangered the house.

Then Beth ordered Baked Gruyère Cheese Soufflé
with ginger root, cauliflower and spinach.

And Tom chose Leg of Lamb with clapshot potatoes,
baby beetroot, and home-made mint sauce.

Religion

Blithely, the stranger on the soapbox claimed
that God was created when they prayed;
that, at night, mystic lights magnified the church,
the abandoned one at the top of the hill.

'Go, at midnight,' he said, 'hear organ music
and ecstatic voices as pure as angels'.'
So they obeyed and climbed the hill of lampposts,
afraid they might find the proof they hoped for.

But the windows were dark and no voices sang.
The doors opened to the muteness of stone
and, relieved, they fell to their knees and prayed.

Song: Yes

Yes to busy music that bullies,
employs your feet, makes you sing;
first love, love that is brief,
shaken–daffodil season,
consummate picture of Spring.

Yes to tra-la-la summer music
pastoral–rich, score unsigned;
sunflower triumphant,
a surprising lit window
before the drawing of a blind.

Yes to grand brooding symphonies
of Berlioz or Mahler;
autumn's fire with chorus,
flowers solemnly dying
in the funeral parlour.

And yes to snow-bleak adagios
that hold the old in thrall
till their chilling pictures fade
and hooks alone are hanging
on a white and vacant wall.

So put your arms about your love
as if she were Molly Bloom
and let your seed-cake kisses be
all the seasons' yes of music
and yes and yes beneath the moon.

Valediction

In this exile people call old age
I live between nostalgia and rage.
This is the land of fools and fear.
Thanks be. I'm lucky to be here.